Success Mantras

Achieve Your Goals

Written by
Kantamneni Radhakrishnamurthy

Translated by
Ms. N. Sharmila Rani

Published by:

F-2/16, Ansari road, Daryaganj, New Delhi-110002
☎ 23240026, 23240027 • *Fax:* 011-23240028
info@vspublishers.com • www.vspublishers.com

Online Brandstore: amazon.in/vspublishers

Regional Office : Hyderabad
5-1-707/1, Brij Bhawan (Beside Central Bank of India Lane)
Bank Street, Koti, Hyderabad - 500 095
☎ 040-24737290
vspublishershyd@gmail.com

Follow us on:   

BUY OUR BOOKS FROM: AMAZON FLIPKART

ISBN 978-93-505702-7-2
New Edition

Printed at : Param Offsetters, Okhla, New Delhi–110020

Contents

Section - III

Section - I
Character Management

Character – An Investment to Success

To be successful in life is everyone's natural desire. Achieving Success means getting something desired or planned in the field one chooses and then moving forward to be ahead from others.

Success gives you the following advantages:

- Recognition in the Society
- Respect and Regard
- When a successful person attends a function or a gathering, he is recognised by all without any introductions
- One can earn money and it provides him comforts and conveniences
- Society remembers him for a long time

However, achieving success is not an easy task. One has to work hard, face difficult situations, hardships and should be disciplined.

Amitabh Bachchan, Kapil Dev, Sunil Gavaskar, Sachin Tendulkar, Dhirubhai Ambani, Steven Spielberg, Ram Gopal Varma, Mani Ratnam, R.D Burman, A.R Rahman, Steffi Graf, Madhuri Dixit, etc are some of the many well-known personalities who belong to different fields but have one aspect or quality common in all of them and that is Success! Victory!!

All these people are successful in their respective fields and have reached to the highest positions in their lives.

However, one may wonder, what methods did they follow, or what acts did they do to reach to that level??

In fact, when you study the lives of all the above mentioned great personalities, you can notice some common qualities such as –

- They all have a goal in their lives, an ambition. Until they achieve their ambition, they do not rest.
- They have a strong personality to face any difficult situation or problem in their path of achieving success.
- They are not overwhelmed with trivial initial results and struggle till the end until they achieve complete success.
- They set a plan and move forward until they achieve their goal.
- They are all workaholics, and follow the principle, 'Work is Worship'.

All the above-mentioned achievers of success are Genius! And we all know that some may be born Genius, but most of them are not born Genius, but made.

When we talk of a Genius, we immediately recall Einstein, one of the greatest scientists of the world. Here's an amazing story behind his genius.

One day some scientists met Einstein and asked his permission to examine his brain after his death. He accepted their request with a small condition.

The condition was that he wanted to place a letter in a sealed cover which was to be opened only after receiving the report prepared on his brain examination!

They accepted his condition.

Later, Einstein passed away. Scientists conducted a thorough examination of his brain and prepared a report, and then they remembered his letter and opened it before all.

There were two sentences written in Einstein's own handwriting:

First sentence – "You have examined my Brain? My brain has nine billion cells like other human brains."

Yes, even the scientists' report said so.

Second sentence –"I alone know what the difference between others and me is."

When they read those two sentences, they were astonished.

Actually, what Einstein intended to say was that he had the same brain what others have, but the only difference was that he had sharpened it with constant use, logical thinking and experimentation.

That is why Intellectuals say that if you want to become a genius, you need 80% perspiration, and 10% inspiration.

Perspiration means–determination, attention, efforts, sincerity and hard work to reach the goal.

To become a genius, or to achieve success in any sphere of life, such as education, profession, love, marriage, etc, one has to put one's efforts or hard work along with the desire and determination to fulfil one's goal. Of course, self-confidence and belief in oneself are compulsory!

In a recent survey conducted in the United States of America, regarding persons who achieved success, or reached to the top in their respective fields revealed that 85% of them attained success by improvising their personalities and the remaining 15% with their experience and talents in their respective fields.

So, in order to succeed, or achieve success in one's field, be it literature, politics, cinema, journalism or any other field, one must first shape one's personality and character. Your personality, character and individuality act as a passport leading your journey towards success. Hence, to achieve shape and groom your character, what all do you have to do??

Here is a famous saying by the well-known scientist, Albert Einstein:

> *"There are only two ways to live your life.*
> *One is as though nothing is a miracle.*
> *The other is as though everything is a miracle."*

You can be adopt any one of the two ways.

Becoming One Among the Two Percent

Many of us do not know the difference between dreaming and making our dreams come true. However, following are six steps to ascend in one's life or career and fulfil one's desires:

1. You have to know what you need, that is your 'Wish' and it is a part of your dream or daydream. This dream does not have any image and about 70% of the world's population are drowning in this daydream.
2. Some people create images of their dreams and change them into 'Desires'. They often think in getting their desires fulfilled but have no commitments in achieving their desires. They end up in just desiring things and almost 10% of the people are of this type.
3. Some people transform their desires into 'Hopes'. They are with the hope and often imagine that by any means their 'Hopes' will be fulfilled. Around 8% of the people are of this type.
4. Some people transform their hopes into 'Belief' and live with the expectation that by any means it will be fulfilled. About 6% of the people are of this type.

5. Few people turn their belief in making their desire come true into 'Burning Desire' and think that it will be definitely fulfilled, and 4% are of this type.
6. Finally, very few ascend to the 4th and 5th steps to fulfil their burning desire to come true, make necessary planning and put cent percent efforts towards it succeeding in the end.

Nothing is impossible for them! But only 2% are of this type.

If you want to become one among the two percent, then read this book until the last page.

Maturity

Any person, if he wants to be a human being should possess a character. To shape the character, first of all, he has to be matured as an individual.

Maturity means a person has to attain perfection physically, mentally, emotionally and in other aspects of life, as well.

One cannot attain maturity in one or two days, it is a continuous process in life.

Physical growth cannot determine the maturity of an individual. It shows only physical maturity. One has to achieve maturity not only physically, but also mentally and in different ways, then only you can say that one has achieved perfect maturity in his personality or character.

Basically, a person has to achieve the following traits to attain perfect maturity:

- **Chronological:** It depends upon how many birthdays you have celebrated.
- **Physical:** When your body has proper and perfect growth, it is physical maturity.
- **Intellectual:** It depends upon how logical and rational your thinking is. This is intellectual maturity.
- **Emotional:** It depends on your feelings and emotions (anger, joy) how you express and release them.
- **Social:** It deals about your social relationship, how correct and pleasant you are able to be with others.
- **Philosophical:** Your philosophical ideals, beliefs, moral values, etc., come under this aspect.

When you achieve perfection in the above mentioned aspects, then only you become a complete man or a woman and can be designated as a matured person.

Now, lets us read each type of maturity in detail:

Chronological Maturity

Your age is calculated from the day when you come out of your mother's womb and how many years, months, days you spend on this earth. Year after year, according to your age, you will become 'older'. If you are born two years earlier than your brother, lifelong, you are two years elder to him. There is no change in it. You cannot increase your age or reduce it.

Chronological Maturity gives certain benefits from the society like right to vote, inheritance right, driving license, right to marry, to open an account in post office or bank etc.....in these situations, chronological maturity helps the individual.

Physical Maturity

If a person attains his complete height, weight and energy, then he is said to have attained physical maturity. For example: A boy, who is in his growing years cannot say his body is physically matured.

When the physical growth stops, it indicates that the person is fully developed or matured. By this time, he receives the energy to do things, which adults usually do without fatigue. The glands in his body function just like the ones in adults.

When a child reaches physical maturity, we have some expectations from him/her in academics, when they participate in sports and games, do jobs, take up the family responsibilities, etc. Physical maturity also shows some influence on the relationship within and outside the family members.

Proper nutrition and exercises also help to some extent in the physical development, but cannot rectify the birth disorders and disabilities.

Intellectual Maturity

There are no measures to weigh whether a person has intellectual maturity or not. However, the points mentioned below will help you to some extent examine whether a person has attained intellectual maturity or not.

- ❑ When he is able to understand the society in which he lives, the cultured words, numbers, signs and is able to respond and communicate with others.

- Taking independent decisions without waiting for others- intellectual maturity is possible only when a person is capable of taking decisions independently.
- When he is able to solve his problems impartially and examine them practically.
- When he makes a mistake and accepts it in a dignified manner, without holding others responsible.

Quick decisions without thinking the outcome of its results is a sign of childish mentality and this shows that the person lacks intellectual maturity.

Intellectual maturity changes from person to person and depends upon the situation in which he is. Another important aspect is that there is a similar relationship between emotional maturity and intellectual maturity.

Emotional Maturity

To get irritated and feel sick when something that we think to happen does not happen and unable to control the anger are human weaknesses. These are the reactions of the people, who lack emotional maturity.

If one achieves the points mentioned below, he will become mentally stable and can attain emotional maturity.

- Accepting the Responsibilities
- Ability to Share the Love with others, as he desires to receive it from others
- One should not always think that his wishes will be fulfilled immediately, but should realise that it takes a lot of time, efforts and determination to fulfil one's desire, and patiently wait until the time comes.

One should reveal only some of his feelings to others and the rest of his feelings must be kept within him. When a person achieves this control over his feelings, he is said to have attained emotional maturity.

Emotional Maturity does not come in one or two days, it develops gradually, and then you have a total control on all your feelings or emotions.

One who achieves emotional maturity stands as a charming personality in the society and the society too compliments him or her.

Social Maturity

Mingling with different people without forming opinions about them comes under social maturity.

The cordial relationship with the society expands wider and stronger when a child becomes a boy, a boy becomes a teenager, and a teenager grows into an adult.

When one leaves his adolescence and enters into an adult life, one needs acquaintances with many different types of people. Therefore, when one deals with others in different situations, he/she has to make many adjustments.

Adjusting with others, without any rivalry and becoming one among others are the qualities of social maturity.

Your achievements like success, popularity, satisfaction, etc., all depend upon your social maturity.

Philosophical Maturity

Every man in his life has a philosophy, which is necessary. Essential values of life, goals, true friends, meaning towards life, dedication, etc -- are all part and parcel of philosophy. When a person attains this philosophical level, it results in philosophical maturity.

This philosophy relates to life, and has to be within the range one lives with the society's terms and conditions, values, family and religion. How close his philosophy agrees with the principles of the society depends upon the philosophical maturity he has attained.

Now examine yourself and find out in how many above said aspects you are matured....

3

Self-Love

(The foundation to build up your Self-Confidence)

It is natural that everyone likes to get love, affection and honour from others. One who does not desire these things from others may be considered a fool or innocent or a sage.

A person should possess an attraction or 'charisma' to receive the desired love, affection and honour from others.

How can one acquire this charisma? What are the efforts one should put in to attain charisma?

Begin it with self-love!!

One who loves himself has a good opinion upon himself. One who has a good opinion upon himself feels that the persons around him also like him and honour him.

When you feel others like you, you will react to them positively. When you react to them in a positive manner, they will also react in the same way and like you.

This kind of giving and taking is called as positive attitude.

The central idea behind all this is self-love and making the people around you to love you.

First Step towards Self-Confidence

Self-love results in self-confidence. Your body complexion, features, personality, stature, and all such aspects depend upon the love and positive attitude you have towards yourself and how much confident you are in your physical appearance.

It is not necessary that all these qualities should be in-built in you. You can achieve them by grooming and self-training yourself. However, to attain self-confidence, it is important by all means to love yourself!!

The famous English writer, 'Oscar Wilde' had once said:

"When one loves himself, it is the foundation for lifelong romance."

It you want to love yourself, you should have a good opinion upon yourself and on your self-image. You can check it by attempting the self-love quiz given in this same chapter.

If you get 35 marks in this self-love quiz, then you are a fairly confident person, particularly, you should know what you are actually thinking and feeling about each part of your body.

Stand Naked before the Mirror

Stand naked before a full size mirror. Now examine each part of your body. It is called as *mirror test*.

Hair	Face	Nails
Body Complexion	Neck	Sense organs
Eyes	Shoulders	Thighs
Ears	Spine	Calves
Eyebrows	Chest	Ankles
*Teeth	Hands	Feet
Lips	Stomach	Toes
Mouth	Lips	etc....
Chin	Fingers	

It should not be Narcissism

Self-love should not be in extreme. If it is extreme, it results in Narcissism. There is a beautiful story in Greek Mythology on Narcissism!

There was a handsome young man called Narcissus. He was so handsome that he used to forget himself by looking at his handsome figure. It made him to develop extreme love and affection upon himself.

Once he sat beside a pool and looked at his shadow with extreme admiration. He tried to catch his shadow (image) in the water and bent forward and drowned.

This is an example of extreme self-love.

First, write about all your body parts separately. Then find out how to know your love towards each part, whenever you look at yourself on the mirror.

Do in the Following Manner

Write your opinion regarding each part, whether you are satisfied or dissatisfied with the part.

It is definite that you love all the parts that give you satisfaction.

Note down all the parts separately that give you dissatisfaction on a paper and you should be careful about these parts.

Now think how you can rectify the defects of those body parts that give you dissatisfaction, for example:

If you are short, you can cover up by wearing shoes with high heels or vertical striped clothing.

* It you have a big stomach or if you feel dissatisfied with any body part, you can rectify it through exercise and suitable makeup.

Self- Love Quiz

Answer the following statements:

1. I like to have myself photographed. 1 2 3 4
2. I will always tell my original age. 1 2 3 4
3. I will cover my grey hair. 1 2 3 4
4. I wish that I may be noticed by everyone. 1 2 3 4
5. I like to introduce the programmes on the stage. 1 2 3 4
6. I like to be stylish. 1 2 3 4
7. Often I check my weight. 1 2 3 4
8. I do not feel shy to run naked on the beach. 1 2 3 4
9. I do the exercise regularly. 1 2 3 4
10. I do not hesitate to take bath in an open place. 1 2 3 4
11. I don't have any inferiority regarding my organs. 1 2 3 4
12. I do not wish about any part of my body to be in another shape 1 2 3 4

If your answer is 'no' for any of the above question, mark '1' if you answer is 'yes', mark '5'. If you feel 25 % 'yes', mark '2' if 50 % yes, then mark '3', and if 75% 'yes' then mark '4'.

Now look at your marks:

Between 36 and 60:

You have complete confidence on your body and feel proud of it.

Between 26 and 35:

You are happy with your body. You do not have any objection to show it before others. However, you like to make some changes regarding some aspects.

Between 12 and 25:

You are not at all happy with your body. You would like to make many changes in your body.

In this manner, if you can rectify the dissatisfied body parts that can be rectified, one by one slowly, after some time, you will love yourself and improve self-confidence.

Many of Them Hate Their Physical Form

We spend most of the time feeling dissatisfied that we should be like some other person than what we are. One-third of the persons in the world have this same opinion (Both ladies and gents).

- This dissatisfaction results in hatred towards your own self and it this tendency is a bit high in females.
- A journal 'Psychology Today' conducted a survey and reported that 75% males and 93% females are dissatisfied with their physical forms.
- This dissatisfaction is because of a hefty personality and overweight. About 41% males and 55% females have been found to be showing their dissatisfaction in this aspect.
- In the above-mentioned survey, half of the males and females complained about their large bellies.
- Ladies often worry about their size of their breasts and buttocks.
- Another amusing fact is that the persons who had satisfaction or dissatisfaction towards their bodies in their teenage continued the same satisfaction or dissatisfaction throughout their later life.
- Around 87% males and 78% females expressed that they feel their bodies were not as attractive in their later age as it were in their teenage.

Therefore, cheer up, since you are not the only one who has dissatisfaction with your physical form, about 75% of the people around you are also of the same opinion...

Pleasant Personality

Primarily, any person in order to show 'himself' as a highly regarded person in the society, should possess a 'personality'. It should be a matured personality-socially, mentally, physically, emotionally, intellectually, etc to achieve perfection in one's personality.

If any person wants to prove or get appreciated in the society, his personality needs an "Aura" –Appearance – then only he gets the right to say proudly, "I am".

Then he does not need any introduction about himself, others recognise him and talk about him in the highest degree.

To achieve a pleasant personality, one should have the qualities mentioned below -

- ❑ Neat Appearance
- ❑ Positive Attitude
- ❑ Reacting according to the Situation
- ❑ Truthful Life
- ❑ Timely Decisions
- ❑ Respect and Regard
- ❑ Witty Conversation
- ❑ Melodious Voice
- ❑ Laughter
- ❑ Patience and Persistence
- ❑ Not Lying
- ❑ Sense of Humour
- ❑ Just Behaviour
- ❑ Controlling the Emotions
- ❑ Concern and Appreciation towards Life
- ❑ Acquiring Knowledge
- ❑ Love and Care for others
- ❑ Not to be Stubborn, Boastful and Proud
- ❑ Sportiveness
- ❑ Good Handshake and Pleasant Speaking

Now examine and self-evaluate yourself to find out how many of the above-mentioned qualities are in you!

Self-Esteem

Say immediately:

Of all, whom do you like the most?

Say quickly:

Not praise-not respect-not love

"Like"

Which person do you like the most?

Is it difficult?

Are you thinking whom you like the most?

Do not worry, the answer is very simple--

The person whom you like the most in this world is- **yourself!!**

Some more questions:

- Are you sad thinking that you are not beautiful?
- Have you thought any time about yourself that "I am fit for nothing?"
- Do you fear that you cannot achieve what you want to achieve?
- Often do you compare with others and feel sad?
- Do you blame yourself when things go wrong?
- Are you always depressed?
- Do you always feel sad about the things, which do not happen, according to your will and about the life, which is not in your control?

If you say, 'Yes' to any one of the above-mentioned questions, then the '**Self-Esteem**' about yourself is very low.

Having high regard upon yourself is called as '**Self-Esteem**' or '**Soul Esteem**'.

Self-Love, Self-Respect, fulfilling the needs, and feeling high about yourself- are some of the qualities of self-esteem!

For example –

If a boy is in deep love with a girl, to look at her, to be near her, or to talk to her… all these things will give him immense happiness. She will be the most important person for him in the world and he will be ready to do anything, or any kind of adventure for her. Isn't it?

Now imagine yourself in the girl's place. Do all the above mentioned activities for yourself instead of the girl and this is called self-esteem!

Self-Esteem influences our thoughts, words, deeds, the way we look at the world, our position in the world, the way we react with others, and finally, it also influences on every decision that we take regarding our lives. It even greatly influences the aspects like 'To Love' and 'To be Loved'.

The Real Test for Self-Esteem

If we are able to love and respect ourselves, even when everything in life turns upside down and our life is almost ruined, that is real self-esteem!

These qualities show that you have self-esteem- patting yourself even when you are in sorrows and sufferings and by not losing the love, respect and high regard upon yourself.

Self- Esteem will be in a higher range in the person who achieves success in every aspect of his life. Such people achieve success through self-love and feel high about themselves. Achievements of success increase the Soul-Esteem in them.

Rooted in Childhood

In every person, Self-Esteem is rooted in his/her childhood. Of all the parts in our body, our brain develops faster! When a child comes into the word from the mother's womb, the size of the brain is generally one/eighth portion of an adult's brain and reaches to half of the size of the adult's brain when they he/she is one and a half years old. When the child reaches five years, the size of the brain grows and develops to become three/fourth of an adult's brain.

During the childhood when the brain grows faster, the imprints of experiences and emotions are rooted strongly in the brain. Later, it is very difficult to erase them.

That is why the bringing up of a child by his/her parents till the age of five influences his/her mind which imprints and remains forever in his/her later lives, especially it highly influences the values that he/she develops upon him/her. These values build up his/her self-esteem.

If the parents bring up their children in a rejected manner or treat them low, then the children feel that they are inferior to other children and the same feeling lasts in them for long even when they grow up into adults. This is one of the main reasons why some people develop a low Self-Esteem or inferiority complex.

Parents can scold their children for their bad or foolish deeds, but they should not make them responsible and hurt their personal feelings.

For example, if a child did not do a given work properly, you should not say, "You are a useless fellow, you can't do any work."

You can instead say, "It would have been better if you had done like this. This is the first time. Next time, you can do it correctly."

You should not use the words like 'unworthy fellow' or 'unfortunate fellow'. These words make the child to think low of him/her leading to inferiority complex.

Self-Confidence and Self-Esteem

Some of them think that self-confidence and self-esteem are one and the same, but it is not correct. Even a person with low self-esteem can move forward with self-confidence in a particular aspect or in a particular thing. Likewise, a person with high self-esteem may lack the self-confidence regarding a particular aspect.

For example, a person with high self-esteem may lack the self-confidence to speak in public places, gatherings, give debates and lectures, etc. He may also be less confident in performing on a stage, playing music, or singing, painting, dancing, etc.

Basically, your mind is like a muscle.

The more you use and-

The more you sharpen it-

It becomes all the more stronger.

Self-confidence means to believe that you can face or solve any problem in any situation with your talents! On the other hand, as a person if you have a high regard upon yourself in the depth of your heart, it is called as **self-esteem!**

If you have a positive or a high regard upon yourself, you can exhibit self-confidence in different situations using your different skills easily. This is the difference between the two.

To simplify it one can say: **Self-Esteem is the foundation for Self-Confidence!**

Inferiority Complex

Inferiority Complex is completely the opposite of Self-Esteem. Some parents always compare their children with their equals or with their brothers or sisters and blame them. Due to this, the child always compares himself with others of his/her age group whom he/she admires and feels low of himself or herself. This makes him to develop a low self-esteem and ultimately, he/she begins suffering from an inferiority complex.

When a child's brain is in the developing stage, this type of foolish behaviour or actions of the parents can even make the child lose belief and respect upon himself destroying his personality and ultimately ruining his life. It may also result in lack of self-esteem and self-confidence and a permanent inferiority complex develops within him.

Behaviour of the Self-Esteemed

The behaviour and the qualities of the self-esteemed are as follows:

- ❑ He feels that he is a prominent and valuable person.
- ❑ He thinks that he has a quality that is respected by others.
- ❑ He can influence others.
- ❑ He thinks and speaks positively about others.
- ❑ He feels and behaves comfortably before his superiors and higher officials without shyness and fear.
- ❑ He is capable of doing his work without caring others' remarks.
- ❑ He takes up responsibilities. If he speaks anything by mistake, he politely agrees and does not try to avoid it and says, "Sorry, I shouldn't have said like that, etc."
- ❑ He values others', opinions and says, "Yes, what you said is correct."
- ❑ If he dislikes a person, he will be away from him or her, but he doesn't pretend and talk to him sweetly with jealousy at heart.
- ❑ When others make negative comments, which are not correct, he tries to defend them.

- He expects others to agree and respect him.
- He works hard in urgent situations.
- He is ready to extend his sympathies and cooperation when needed.
- He never boasts of himself.
- He is always ready to praise the righteousness, capabilities and greatness in others.

To sum up in brief, we can say that a person who has self-esteem is liberal and very generous!

The more you like and respect yourself,

The more you like and respect others.

Likewise, others also like and respect you!

The Behaviour of a Person with Low Self-Esteem

Self-esteem is very high in some persons and is very low in some people. If we take a scale of Zero to Ten, 'very low' is Zero and 'very high' is 'ten', then the persons in between these numbers have different levels of self-esteem.

On the scale, if it shows Zero, the self-esteem is very low and of negative quality and if it shows Ten, then the self-esteem is very high and of positive quality.

The behaviour of the persons who have self-esteem between 5 and 10 on the scale are considered to be average and good.

If the scale indicates zero, it shows not only a very low self-esteem, but also an inferiority complex in a person.

Now let us examine the behaviour of the people who have a low self-esteem or **Inferiority Complex!**

Healthy Personality

Many people in the world think that they have a 'Healthy Personality' or they want to have a healthy personality.

What is the definition for a 'Healthy Personality'?

A healthy personality has three important qualities:

- The first quality of a Healthy Personality is looking 'comfortable and good' in every situation and facing each situation that we encounter in life bravely. Looking 'uncomfortable and bad' in every situation is the symptom of an'Unhealthy Personality'.
- The second quality of a Healthy Personality is to excuse the persons who have harmed and distressed you! You will lose

your peace and happiness if you always think of the harm they made to you. If you forgive them, the mind will also be free. The persons who have a healthy personality do not keep their anger, hatred, dislike and revenge in their minds. They do not worry about the past things and always erase those memories from their minds. Forgiveness always keeps the minds calm and clear.

- The third quality of a Healthy Personality is to mix with the people who are with different mentalities, attitudes and motives! It is easy to mix with the people who have same opinions, likes and dislikes and are equal in their economical and social aspects. But it is impossible for all to live together and mix with the people who have different opinions, values, personalities, temperaments, etc. Only the persons who have a healthy personality can do it. The third quality is the most important milestone for a healthy personality!

Measure

Self-Esteem is the measure for a Healthy Personality. The more you like and respect yourself, the more you like and respect others and likewise, others also like and respect you!

If you value yourself, then others also start valuing you.

The persons with low self-esteem show more anger, intolerance, irritation and indulge in loose talk. They become a nuisance to the people around them. They do not like themselves or others. As a result, others also do not like them. These are the symptoms of an unhealthy personality.

Improvement of '**Self-Esteem**' leads to a '**Healthy Personality**'!

Throwing Blame upon Others

The people without self-esteem try to put the blame upon others if any calamity or loss occurs in their lives. They never accept the truth that the loss has occurred because of their defect or mistake.

They feel happy and comfortable when they hold others responsible for their failures. It also shows that others are inferior to them.

The self-esteemed (*soul-esteemed*) take up the responsibility for the loss and act in a decent manner.

Finding Faults

The people without self-esteem always try to find fault with others, particularly to hide their own faults from others. For example, a woman who is herself at fault tries to find fault with other women. She is only interested in useless gossips.

Curious about Others' Compliments

Many people try to attract others' attentions and care a lot about others' opinions. They try their level best to get compliments from others and all these are because of not having enough confidence on their own merits and values.

In other words, persons without self-esteem always struggle for others' compliments. They try to cover up their own follies and defects through others' good or bad remarks.

Self-boasting and Speaking High

Some people always talk high and boast about themselves. This shows their inferiority complex. Those who have no self-esteem cover their own faults in this way and deceive themselves and others by such things, i.e., self-boasting!

In order to make an impression on others that they are valuable, they say, "I can do like this, or I can do like that."

They behave like this because they have no confidence and honour upon themselves and think that others also have the same feeling about them.

These are the symptoms of Inferiority Complex!

It is natural to compare ourselves with others.

But 'winners' never compare with others.

In their opinion, 'success' means to perform the 'best'

in them, according to the standards they set!

Winners accept 'themselves' as they are and keep moving forward

making continuous and necessary changes in them for their self-development.

Unable to Resist Compliments

Some people feel shy when others praise them. This also shows their lack of self-esteem! For example, if a man wears a new shirt, and you say, "This is very nice," "where did you buy from?" If he replies, "I didn't like it but there wasn't another one to buy in that shop, so I bought this one," or "this is not even of the latest fashion." These kinds of replies reveal that he lacks self-esteem. However, if he replies, "Thank you" or "I searched four or five shops and brought this and I too liked it."- This expression shows that he has a high self-esteem!

So also, when a student is congratulated for passing in first class and if he says, "It's all God's grace" or "because my father compelled me to read, that's why I got this rank," shows that he does not know his own value.

But if he answers that "I worked hard throughout the year and I succeeded," then we can make out that he is crowned with self-esteem.

These types of reactions when praised by others stand as a milestone for self-esteem!

Do you know the great wealth of a person?

Self-Esteem upon himself,

Self-Respect upon himself and

Personal Pride upon himself.

Do you know the foundation for all this?

Self-Confidence in himself!

Addicted to Bad Habits

We see some people who are addicted to drinking and taking drugs. These people also do not have confidence or respect upon themselves.

These addictions can be of different types. For example: Excessive eating, drinking, addiction to drugs, gambling, excessive smoking, etc. in order to forget one's psychological agony and overcome the emotional distress and inability to accept and respect oneself. Such people get addicted to such things for temporary relief.

Unable to take Decisions, Postpone the Work

Some people who have no self-esteem fear that they may commit mistakes. They feel that whether they can do the work or not, whether they can live up to the expectations or not. With these thoughts, they go on postponing their work until it becomes too late.

Sometimes, they even postpone taking decisions thinking that they can't do the work in a proper way.

So also, a perfectionist who wants to do every work without any defect and be perfect, comes under the category of the low self-esteemed. They like to do every work too perfect.

The reason for this is that they have a feeling of insecurity in their minds, which caution them to be away from criticism. By postponing the work and by not doing the work at all, they try to be away from criticism.

If they have high regard upon themselves, they do the work without postponing and think that "I completed the work according to my best of abilities."

The persons with low self-esteem have the following emotional, physical and psychological characteristics:

Emotional

- To be aggressive
- Feels shy
- Laughs forcefully
- Boasts about oneself
- No patience at all
- Wants to take an 'upper hand'
- Headstrong
- Always tries to satisfy others
- Always criticises others
- Revolts against the authorities
- Wants everything to be perfect
- Wants to dominate others
- Interferes in the middle when others are talking
- Postpones the work
- Never accepts his/her faults
- Addicted to drinking and smoking

Physical

- Droops physically
- No grip in handshake, likes to be alone
- Blank expression
- Bulky body
- Seems to be nervous and tensed
- Not neatly dressed
- Feeble voice
- Unable to look into the eyes of others

Psychological

- Anxious
- Dislike upon himself/herself
- Thinks that others should like him or her or accept him/her
- Always with an unstable mind

- Considers himself as an unlucky fellow
- Reacts to insult, crime and repentance
- Always wants to be 'correct'
- Always with troubles
- Thirst of power, money and status

All the above are some of the bad qualities due to lack of self-esteem.

Not that all these qualities may not be together in a person who lacks self-esteem, but he can have any one quality or a combination of some of the above mentioned qualities.

There is a popular saying:

"If you think you can, you can. And if you think you can't, you're right."

– Mary Kay Ash

The essence is that one must be clear in one's mind and bold in one's thoughts and expressions as to what one desires and what one expresses.

Skilful Conversation

Skilful Conversation is an art. It will help us to please others and make them to be on our side. Skilful Conversation means knowing what to talk, how to talk,when to talk, and what not to talk with others! It is also known as tact. The persons, who do not have tact, speak in the following ways. In other words, if you want to be tactful, don't talk and behave in the following ways:

- Coarse voice, Negligence
- Speaking useless talk when one has to be silent
- Interfering when others talk
- Boasting about 'you' always
- Asking unnecessary questions to exhibit your knowledge
- Causing inconvenience to others by speaking about their personal matters
- Going to places without invitations
- Speaking high about yourself
- Not dressing according to the situation
- Knocking doors or making phone calls during odd hours
- Wasting others' time by speaking unnecessary matter over the phone
- Writing letters on personal matters to persons who are not much familiar

- ❑ Giving free advices regarding matters which you don't know
- ❑ Not accepting or making fun of others' opinions
- ❑ Giving headstrong answers to others' questions
- ❑ Talking low of a person in front of his friends
- ❑ Teasing persons who do not agree with you
- ❑ Passing comments on the disabilities and defects of people
- ❑ To comment on the faults and mistakes of your colleagues and subordinates, in front of all
- ❑ To disclose a confidential matter to everyone
- ❑ Always pleading your friends for help
- ❑ Making others angry by using foul language
- ❑ To show your dislike and anger towards others on trivial matters
- ❑ To complain everybody about the sickness and misfortunes of your life
- ❑ Always showing your resentment on religious matters and politics
- ❑ To be close with everybody unnecessarily

The above mentioned things may look very small, but in fact, these are the things that make others to have a cheap impression about you. So, a person who aspires for a healthy personality should be away from all the above mentioned qualities.

How to Improve Self-Esteem

(Self-Esteem Tips)

The most important and primary quality of a person to achieve success is Self-Esteem! The qualities of self-esteem are self-respect, to respect yourself and to believe on your worth.

Self-confidence is easily fixed in the mind of a person who has self-esteem. To think high about you should be like a feeling rather than an idea or an opinion! This is the real self-esteem.....

There are people who do not know the real reason that many problems, which they face in their lives, directly or indirectly arise because of low self-esteem.

To love and respect yourself is self-esteem!

For example: One fine morning, if God appears and asks you, "Do you want to change your life and for that do you need any boon?" And if you reply with all your heart, "No Lord, my life is wonderful, I feel happy and satisfied with my parents and my social background. I am not thinking to be born in another age or in another world. This life is sufficient." Then the self–esteem in you is immeasurable!

Particularly, you have immense self-esteem when you say the above sentences in your poverty or distress, etc.

It is easier to recognise the person without self-esteem. For example, a person who speaks in a loud voice just like shouting has low self-esteem. These types of persons are compared with a fellow called John Dillinger. Here goes the story of John Dillinger:

A fellow called John Dillinger entered into a home with a gun, fired four rounds in the air and frightened the ten persons who gathered there. He said like this:

"My name is John Dillinger. I came here to tell my name but not to harm you or to frighten you. Remember my name..."

Psychologists compare the persons who speak loudly with John Dillinger.

The most important requirement for self-confidence is self-esteem. Self-esteem, if strongly fixed in the mind will be useful to bring the following habits into your life.

Neat Dressing

Neat dressing has also been discussed in this book under the head, **'Conduct Management'**. By going through the following passage, you can understand the importance of neat dressing in your life. Do a small experiment.

One day you go to the market wearing an old shirt, which is not ironed, folded and faded.

Next day, go to the same market wearing a correct fitted new dress.

In both the above situations, observe your own feelings rather than how others are watching you.

When you wear folded clothes, you feel in your heart that something lacks in you and you are inferior to the people around you.

When you wear correct fitted, ironed clothes, you feel happy and superior to the people around you.

The clothes we wear have much importance. The reason for this is –

There is a strong relationship between the mind and the body. When we eel emotionally sad or sorrowful, our body becomes dull. We do not care bout the dressing and appearance at that time.

So also physically, when we suffer from a disease or injury, there may ot be quickness in our thinking. We, generally get negative thoughts.

Likewise, when we are neatly dressed, deep in our hearts, we feel very appy. We think about ourselves in a positive manner. Subconsciously, we orm a high regard upon ourselves.

Basically, these are the some of the main aspects to achieve confidence nd success.

In this regard, a survey was also made by the Harvard University which evealed that the people, who feel that they are not attractive and beautiful and without friends are suffering from loneliness, and even their friends, many times reject them.

It is also said that the school-going children who are cheerful and charming are receiving love and affection not only from their friends and family, but also from their teachers.

Accept Yourself

The most important aspect to develop self-esteem is to accept yourself!

Even if you have any physical disability, if you are not good looking, if you don't have intelligence, or if you are in poverty, in all these situations, you have to accept yourself.

This means, in spite of your physical disability or background, you have to love yourself and accept yourself.....

Nature gave you life, the body, the blood in your body, emerging thoughts in your brain and its vivacity, and all these are the gifts of nature. Even if you have any defect in any part of your body, don't hate it.

Just like distant objects are clear, don't feel jealous of others' qualifications and qualities which you don't have.

Yours is yours!

Self-esteem develops in you when you try to set right your defects by loving and accepting yourself.

Set Down Some Standards for You

Never compare yourself with others. Never think of their comforts and victories.

You are a special person. By birth or by nature, you are having some boundaries and limitations and you have to obey them, isn't it??

Set down some ideal standards. **How to lead your life, How to behave What to achieve in your profession, How to maintain relations with others, etc. Try your level best to achieve these standards systematically.**

By doing this, you can improve your character and self-respect.

Self-Esteem

Have you ever seen a person who cannot be alone for a moment?

Actually, the persons who don't have self-respect upon themselves can't be alone, they need someone around them in order to feel their presence.

Sad part is that others do not like the persons who want to be in the midst of the others! Who will respect the persons who don't have self-respect upon themselves?

Therefore, it is very important that the person first needs self-respect upon himself or herself.

Observe the behaviour and qualities of a person that you like the most and the persons whom you are familiar with. Inculcate those qualities in you and in your life. Self-respect increases in you automatically.

Make Rational Thinking

Many of them take hasty decisions emotionally and get biased. It is not correct.

Emotions always suppress the acquired knowledge to come forth. They won't let your brain think rationally. This may result in taking wrong decisions.

It is also not correct to be without emotions. Without emotions, there is no excitement, diversity in life. Life will become arid and dull.

Like children, we have to enjoy the emotions like love, compassion, joy, grief and sorrow. While taking the decisions regarding life, they must be rational combined with logic and common sense. It means the decisions have to be taken only after soothing down your anger.

Read Biographies

Whenever you find time read the life histories of the prominent persons. They can be the Biographies and Autobiographies of writers, artists, politicians, etc...

Especially autobiographies are very useful, because they contain honesty and truth in them.

We can find many books on autobiographies and biographies in English. By reading the life histories of Mahatma Gandhi, Charlie Chaplin, Maxim Gorky, etc we can know how they overcame the struggles and difficulties in their life and reached to the high position. We can also understand that they are also like us and they too have weaknesses like us. It gives us an inspiration and self-confidence.

When we read of the "weaknesses of those prominent persons", this knowledge helps us to build confidence in us even if we have any low self-esteem upon us. This is an essential quality to achieve self-esteem!

Don't Tell Lies

By telling lies, you lose self-respect. If you are a liar, whenever you tell lies to others, it is natural that you feel bad deep down in your heart. Because of this unknowingly, you form a low impression upon yourself.

But one thing is sure that in this modern, world it's impossible to live without telling a lie. In some unavoidable situations, when a lie repairs the life of a person or if it does some good to him, such 'emergency lies', or 'harmless lies' can be accepted.

Even when we live without using these kinds of lies, it's great that we form a high self-respect, upon us!

Play with Children

Nothing is so sacred and wonderful than childhood. **It is like a special classroom that gives training to change as Adults!** There is a lot to learn from our childhood and that's why whenever you find leisure, play with children. Make them to smile, laugh and play. Listen to their conversation and their dreams. Observe their special talents. Ask about their humorous opinions and reactions.

When you spend time amidst their innocent laughter and talk, you feel that you have spent your time in a fantasy world.

Spending time with children refreshes the mind.

Spend Half an Hour for Yourself Everyday

Daily, when you wake up in the morning, allot half an hour exclusively for you.

After you wake up, without getting down from the bed, lie down for half an hour or sit in a yogic posture. Remember the day's work and plan to do them in your best way.

Remember, it's your life, and how to lead it in an honest and disciplined manner is in your hands. Every morning, think of it, how to live and behave.

Whatever you do and however you behave, finally, you have to decide and prosper. Your self-respect should not reduce.

Showing Interest towards Life

Show interest towards your life, read books, listen to music, etc.

Whenever you find time, embark on short journeys. Observe the people in your travel. Talk to them. Look at beautiful places, and enjoy the wonderful monuments, wildlife, birds, sceneries, and many such things.

Observe the diversities and the beauties of the world. Feel happy that you have a place in this beautiful world. This is how you can enjoy your life!

Through this, your mind flourishes, and you develop a broader outlook, healthy thoughts bloom and finally, you enhance your self-respect.

Make Walking a Daily Habit

Daily go for a walk and make it a habit. This will improve your health. Health consultants suggest that walking is the best exercise for good health.

While you walk, recollect the past memories of your childhood. Your childhood friends, the games you played, the places you travelled, your dreams.......by recollecting all these things not only your mind gets refreshed, but also your memory power sharpens.

Avoid Watching TV

Some people are always glued to the television, or popularly called the 'Idiot Box'. Too much watching of the television (TV) results in many disadvantages, rather than advantages.

Watching TV always results in loss of memory power, particularly among children and a weak eyesight.

Watching selective programmes is fine, but watching all the programmes may spoil the children, particularly, in their growing age.

Listen to Music

Make it a habit to relax daily for some time and listen to the music of your choice. This is good, especially during the night-time before sleep.

Be lonely in your room, switch of the lights and play the music of your choice. Soft and melodious music or Hindustani Classical Music will be effective.

Audio cassettes of Shiv Kumar Sharma's Santoor, Hariprasad Chaurasia's Flute, Ali Akbar Khan's Sarod, Bismillah Khan's Shehnai, etc., are some of the best Indian or Hindustani Classical Music available in the market.

While you listen to music with your mind's eye, imagine different visuals like ricochet of the raindrops falling amongst the leaves of the forest, sound of the sea tide, chirping of birds, a trip in a boat on the river, trickle of water falling from the mountains, sleeping in the lap of your lover, etc.

These visuals sharpen your creativity.....

Try to Understand Others' Perspectives

Before criticising a person or passing judgement on a person, try to look at the problem with his/her eyes. Try to understand the feelings of that person.

Don't forget that as you feel that you're a special person, others also have the same feelings about themselves. Try to understand that when you are in that person's position, how he or she thinks or feels is *Empathy*.

There are two words: *Empathy* and *Sympathy*.

Sharing the feelings of others is *Sympathy*.

Understanding and entering into another's feelings is *Empathy*.

For example:

A person who is participating in a 20 mile-running race, feels pain in his legs when he is ready to reach his last mile. While looking at that person, if you experience the same pain in your legs, it is called Empathy.

Similarly, in the 15th round of the 'Rakhi' movie, Sylvester Stallone was unable to lift up his hands. When you experience the same feeling in your hands, it is Empathy.

Empathy means entering into the mind of the other person and experiencing his/her feelings......

To understand this, ask the following questions to yourself!

"How would I feel if I was my wife and having a husband like me?"

"How would I feel if I was my mother and having a son like me?"

"How would I like if I was my manager and having an employee like me?"

"How would I like if I was my son or daughter having a father like me?"

Understanding others' feelings is Empathy, or looking at others from their point of view.

Empathy helps to bring gentleness into the mind. To exercise this, imagine how does the world look through the eyes of babies!

Be Honest

Honesty is the best policy in a person's character. In your behaviour, there is no 'more honest' or 'less honest' but 'to be honest' or 'to be dishonest'.

Honest persons never fear anybody on any aspect. Because of this, they have a lot of freedom and opportunity to put their energies through artistic efforts. Every person has to be given due prominence to be honest in his life. An honest person has a value and recognition in the society.

If you don't have certainty upon any matter which you know, better don't tell it to anybody. In order to escape from it, don't tell whatever lies that come to your mouth. To cover one lie, one has to tell more lies. So never try to tell lies. By doing so, you are free from worries.

Every man should think from his heart at least once, how honest he is, in not only telling lies but also in longing for others' money, things and women. If the answer is, 'yes' he can be considered as the best citizen who has a high conduct in the society.

There are two things-to be honest or to be dishonest. If you select the first one and practise it strictly, you will not only develop self-esteem, but also earn respect and honour from the society in the long course of time!

Money has no Character

Yes, money has no character, no personality and no values. Works of money reflect its master's wishes or desires.

With money, one can build huge hospitals, schools, museums, gamble and buy weapons of destruction.....

If you earn lots of money, to protect your character and self-esteem, spend some money from your earning to help others.

Provide education for poor students, give alms to orphanages and old age homes......

By doing these kinds of noble deeds, you are the profiteer but not others, your soul is satisfied and your mind feels great about you......

Don't Deceive Yourself

Do you like yourself?

Prove it. If you have proper character, definitely you will respect yourself. Have a clear understanding about your goals, your dreams, and what you want to become in future.

Don't deceive yourself, if you do so, your character begins to degrade. So try to analyse your character logically.

"Am I living as I am or without having own thoughts, acting according to others' advices or wishes?"

"Is my character according to my own will?"

"Do I admire all the qualities in me?"

Ask these types of questions to yourself!

Come to a decision what you want to be and how you want to be. Make a proper planning to reach that destination and behave accordingly. Then you will feel fully satisfied......

Don't Gossip

All persons usually have a limited time, energy and money. Everybody has to be careful while spending these things. One has to be choosy, especially while spending one's time!

So don't sit with idle people and gossip. Don't waste your time by spreading rumours about others, as ultimately, nobody believes these types of persons because......

A person who speaks ill about others will also speak ill about anybody! Everybody knows this fact, so even if they talk to that person politely, inside, in their hearts, they always doubt him/her….

Always Smile

Smile is a universal language, it is a positive language and is a symbol of friendship.

If you smile at a person, it shows you are positive and friendly towards him or her. Your smile brings back the same type of response from others.

Smile means-

"I am 'O.K', are you'O.K'?"

If you are 'O.K', your self-esteem is also 'O.K'!

Walk Straight

Walk looking straight ahead and maintaining a proper posture and distance between your steps. Your walk will improve your self-confidence.

Say, Thank You

If anybody compliments you, without making fuss, simply and politely say, "Thank you!" It shows your confidence in you. If you follow these things properly, you will develop love, confidence, honour and self-esteem.

Self-Confidence

Self-confidence is the knowledge within yourself that you can do something, and do it well or with full confidence in oneself or one's own abilities!

Psychiatrists suggest that if a person lacks self-confidence, irregularities take place in his nature and individuality.

In any person, lack of confidence can be seen of two types:

First type - Lacking confidence, only in some situations and in particular timings.

Second type - Lacking confidence always in life on any matter or in any situation.

For example, lacking confidence in particular situations-

If there is a doctor, he can treat the patients very confidently in a hospital with all specialities. But suddenly to treat a person, who had a severe accident on the roadside and struggling for life and death, the doctor lacks confidence during that situation.

So also, a girl who enjoys talking and playing jokes with her friends will feel shy when she, all of a sudden comes in contact with new persons.

Lacking confidence in particular situations can't be taken seriously. But lacking confidence in all situations and every time shows that the persons have some defects in their individualities.

Such type of people behave horribly and in a strange manner. To them, each and every person seems to be a suspicious character and an enemy.

Fear

In many situations, a person lacks confidence because of fear. This fear may be a natural one or imaginary.

This fear inhibits us to achieve what we want or desire in our lives. In other words-

Fear kills the confidence of a person. If there is no confidence, we cannot achieve anything, whatsoever we want to achieve in our lives!

For instance, we have to do a work and if we are in a confusion whether we can do it or not, then remember an important thing-

Instead of sitting idle in fear or doubt whether we can do it or not, first start the work! By doing the work, we can gradually get rid of the fear.......

There are various types of fears that are common in people. Each person has a different type of fear and each fear has a different reason. According to the reason, each fear has a solution. For example, you have the following types of fears:

- ❑ Fear that you aren't good looking
- ❑ Fear that you may lose customers or your job
- ❑ Fear that what others will think of you
- ❑ Fear to come into the midst of strangers or people whom you dislike

Like these......

In order to get rid of these types of fears, act in the following manner:

- ❑ The persons who fear that they are not good looking can try to look delicate and stylish through suitable dressing and proper makeup.
- ❑ The persons who fear that they will lose their customers or their jobs can put on hard work and upgrade their services.
- ❑ The persons who fear that they may fail in exams have to arrange for a tutor, without wasting time, or they have to utilise the time by concentrating and working hard in their studies.
- ❑ The persons who fear that what others will think of them can come out of it by behaving properly with good moral values without causing any harm to others.
- ❑ The persons who fear to come out and mingle with others have to set aside their shyness. Don't forget that there is a remedy to all sorts of fears. Try to set it right by yourself by becoming more frank and keep aside the shyness. (Also one can read books on 'Self Help' as they are easily available and are in plenty in bookshops!)

Therefore, by following different types of remedies to different types of fears, one can enhance one's self-confidence.

However, the most important thing to remember is that confidence never comes to a person by birth. One can acquire confidence through learning and changing one's lifestyle. And this is the first and foremost quality of wise people.

As there was a Buddha in Siddhartha, a Vivekananda in Narendra, a Mahatma in Mohandas Karamchand Gandhi, so also definitely, there will be a successful person in you excelled in any one field. So it is your duty to search and bring out that successful person in you!!

Behaviour of Confident Persons

A person who has perfect self-confidence possesses the following qualities:

- He has love, respect and confidence upon himself. He never tries to conceal it even if he knows, others are aware of it.
- He is clear about his desires and intentions. In order to achieve his goals, he leads a disciplined life.
- Whenever he faces problems, he is never depressed but tries to think in a positive manner like how to overcome the problems and solve them. He never tries to run away from problems. That's why he has high optimism. This optimism helps him to achieve success in life.
- He knows how to behave in different situations. He possesses skills and cleverness.
- The persons who have self-confidence never believe blindly whatever they listen.

They take independent decisions after an indepth analysis regarding a particular matter.

- The person who has self-confidence never yields to temptations, he stands to his principles, but never boasts.
- He behaves according to his needs and ideals, but never expects compliments from others.
- In order to have an upper hand on others, he never oppresses or talks low about others. Therefore, others also have confidence upon his honesty and respect him.
- The person with self-confidence knows his weaknesses clearly, so he never hesitates to admit his weaknesses before others, even his mistakes.

- He is always calm and relaxed.
- He is ready to change his behaviour according to the situation.
- When he is in need, he never hesitates to receive or to ask help from others.

The reason that you are in the same condition and not progessing in life is:

Not that you lack ability,
Not that you lack opportunities,
But you lack 'Confidence'!

Lack of Confidence

Lack of confidence results in many disadvantages. A person who has no confidence can't achieve any victory and can't complete any work. Many defects take place in his behaviour and nature. For example:

- He can't mingle with others and always remains lonely.
- He behaves nervously and awkwardly.
- He is known as a frightened and timid person.
- Often he feels sick because of constant nervousness and tension.
- His inability makes him to be an unknown and useless person in the society.
- In the course of time, he becomes a pessimist.
- Often he is in depression.

The above mentioned qualities are seen inwardly in some persons and outwardly in some persons.

The behaviour of a self-confident person is dignified, and we feel comfortable when we are beside him. For example:

A Confident Friend

- He never wants everyone to like him because he knows that it is impossible. So he tries to spend his precious time with his dear ones.
- He has friends not only from his own profession, but also from different professions and never thinks that his friends should be like him. He never protests to make friendship with the people who have different tastes and interests.
- He never feels that his friends should have the same ideology like his. He respects their ideologies and values. For example, he can have B.J.P friends with conservative ideals or Communist friends

with radical ideals. He respects their commitments towards their ideologies.

- He has a practical understanding about his friends and never wants them to behave according to his needs. He remains serious with some friends, affectionate with some friends and good-humoured with some friends.
- He knows which friend will help him in his troubles. Even if none of them lends a hand, he never feels hurt or shocked. He takes it in a casual way.
- He never feels displeased when his friends say, "No" to his request and feels that it's their right to accept it or not.
- So also, he never hesitates to say, "No" if he doesn't like anything. He doesn't like to interfere in anybody's personal affairs, whether he/she is his friend or not.
- He never hesitates to pass productive comments when he disagrees with the attitudes and behaviour of his friends.
- He is always ready to face any situation that comes in his life when he is moving ahead. Sometimes, he loses some friends and gains some new friends.
- He never feels sad when he loses his friends or disinterested to make new friends who do not suit his temperament.

A Confident Wife/Husband

- He/she has a clear understanding not only about his/her rights, but also about his/her duties. He/she never tries to escape from his/her duties as husband and wife.
- He/She never shapes his/her household according to his/her expectations, but according to the mentalities and comforts of both.
- He/she shows decency when he/she passes a comment or receives a comment from either of them. He/her realises the truth that his/her relation continues only when the comments are in give and take approach.
- Both husband and wife have to know clearly that their comments have some limitations and these comments should not hurt the 'Ego' of either of them.
- When they are angry, they never hesitate to show that anger on either of them as he/she feels that there is no wrong in doing so.

- ❑ He/She never hesitates to says 'Sorry' when he/she commits a mistake. So also, he/she is ready to excuse the faults of each other in a decent manner.

Are You in an Ideal Profession?

The profession in which you have opportunities to utilise your talents and capabilities completely is called as 'ideal profession'.

Not only this, your boss has to extract work from you. Unfortunately, some wicked bosses who, in order to hide their inferiority complexes at home and frustrations in their personal life very unkindly scream on their subordinates and show hell to them. This sort of professional atmosphere gives unhappiness and tension.

So also, the deceitfulness and jealousy of colleagues makes the profession unpleasant.

In both the above mentioned situations, the profession may be suitable for you, but the work environment is bad.

In order to know whether your profession is giving you satisfaction or dissatisfaction, answer 'yes' or 'no' for the following situations.

- ❑ Daily, when you wake up and remember your work, you feel distressed. ***Yes*** ☐ ***No*** ☐
- ❑ For many years, you are in the same job and same cadre without any promotions. ***Yes*** ☐ ***No*** ☐
- ❑ The profession is always a routine job without any challenge. ***Yes*** ☐ ***No*** ☐
- ❑ Often you think to quit your present job and find a new one. ***Yes*** ☐ ***No*** ☐
- ❑ You have lost your confidence after joining in the job/profession. ***Yes*** ☐ ***No*** ☐
- ❑ There are no opportunities in your profession to use your skills. Even your higher officials are not reacting to your appeal. ***Yes*** ☐ ***No*** ☐
- ❑ You feel bore when you are at office and always look at the watch. ***Yes*** ☐ ***No*** ☐
- ❑ You don't give or have the respect of your colleagues, and don't like their interests and tastes. ***Yes*** ☐ ***No*** ☐
- ❑ You don't understand how your colleagues are enjoying their work. In your office, you feel that you are an outsider. ***Yes*** ☐ ***No*** ☐

- ❑ You don't have a good opinion on the standards and goals of your company or organisation. *Yes* ☐ *No* ☐
- ❑ Recently, you are in romance with your colleague. *Yes* ☐ *No* ☐

Among all the above mentioned situations, if any two or more situations are applicable to you, then you are not in the ideal profession. In such a situation, it is better to change into another profession or job, or start your own business!

A Confident Mother

- ❑ A confident mother, if finds any mistake while fostering her children, is always ready to admit the mistakes and tries to learn a lesson from those mistakes.
- ❑ Her aim is to give complete motherhood to her children, but not wish that her children always honour or praise her.
- ❑ She always remembers that the love and guidance shown upon her children will influence their minds, and so she behaves accordingly.

For example:

- ❑ According to her interests on dressing and appearance, her children also show interest regarding their dressing and appearance.
- ❑ The attachment and relationship with her husband influences the future of her children.
- ❑ She displays decency and valour in her behaviour, and children also display the same.
- ❑ She feels and remains happy, so children also feel happy and acquire the abilities to enjoy life.

Hence, a confident mother is aware of all the above mentioned qualities and behaves accordingly.

- ❑ If she is an employee, she never feels that she is a superwoman and tries to do both the work at home and office. When there is a need, she takes the help of her husband or children at home and her colleagues at office. Whenever she feels tired, she never hesitates to give the duties of the household and childcare to her husband.
- ❑ She never dictates or imposes her likes and dislikes on her children. As a mother, she never misuses her power! She leaves some decisions to the will of her children and gets involved

only when she feels that her children need some experienced advices.

- She never hesitates to enforce discipline and punishment, when she feels that her children are behaving in a wrong manner or going out of control towards the wrong path.
- When she feels that her children have reached a certain age, she does not restrict their independence. Even she allows them to take reasonable risks. She also gives them a chance to learn lessons from their failures.
- She never interferes when her children set some standards and ideals for them, but definitely interferes when those standards and ideals harm the children or others.
- A confident mother tries to take up her own responsibilities in her old age, but never depends upon her children to look after her in her old age! However, during the hour of need, when they come forward to give their help and support, without any hesitation, she receives it.
- While fostering her children, she bears all the distress that she comes across, but never complains or feels that she made sacrifices. She does all the work as part of her responsibilities.
- She allows her children to set up their own lifestyle, but never insists that their lifestyle should be according to her desires, ideals and fantasies.

Self-confidence is a talent which is to be learnt, just like typing and cycling. The more you practise, The more it will get fixed in your mind. Ordinary people have desires and hopes, but the people who have **Self-confidence** have plans to fulfil their goals. Likewise, people who have self-confidence will exhibit maturity by putting in various characters capably in the right place in their lives.

People in any profession or holding any responsibility, having complete confidence upon their work without thinking what others think about them, is called self-confidence!

When a person with self-confidence feels that what he is doing is not correct or good, he immediately abandones and comes out of it. A person who lacks self-confidence continues doing the same wrong thing time and again, and tries to put the blame on others for doing it.

This is the difference between self-confidence and lack of self-confidence.

Sometimes Failures are Necessary

It is natural for all of us to face failures, at least once in our lifetime, especially in today's competitive world as hurdles are definite. So always remember the following facts regarding failures:

- It is natural for any human being to commit mistakes. When you have taken up a work and without completing it, if you end up the work in the middle, you have to learn a lesson from it.
- Never fear failures, they will help you to make certain changes in life and lead you towards progress.
- Failures enable you to know that you are searching happiness in a wrong place with wrong reasons. It makes you to change the direction of your life.
- Accepting failure is the journey towards success.
- We fear failures because we are scared what others will think of us. Nobody bothers about your failures, as you imagine because everyone is busy with his/her own problems.
- Don't look at your failure as a gigantic one. Others' judgements upon you may not be as harsh as you imagine.
- Don't forget that persons who achieve success are bound to face failures sometimes!
- Life is a combination of successes and failures, it is natural and you are not an exception.
- Whenever you self-examine yourself, be careful, never think that "I am unfit," instead you think that "I have given my level best, but some mistakes rolled in."
- When you are unable to do some work, ask the following questions to yourself:
  - "Is there anything that I can do?"
  - "In which areas I can excel?"
  - "What changes can I make to achieve this?"

Remember –Failures show the way to shape your life positively.

Self-Confidence Quiz

To be favourable or unfavourable to the outward circumstances will influence success to some extent.

But some persons with their '**will-power**' bring success into their custodies easily. They have the capacity to mould their lives according to their will. This **will-power** is their **self-confidence**!!

To know how confident you are in your day to day life and to know your confidence levels, write 'yes' or 'no' after the following statements whichever is applicable to you.

You have to write 'yes' or 'no' for the statements honestly. You can exactly know your confidence levels when you honestly mark them.

1. You get into the bus with your mother. There is no space. After standing for some time, you notice some gents sitting in the 'Ladies' seats. You go and ask them to vacate a seat for your mother.
2. You attend a party. After coming back from the party, you blame yourself for not impressing the people with your talk and behaviour.
3. You were asked a question in a group discussion or classroom. You knew the answer but you sat quietly without giving answer.
4. When you attend a meeting or conference, you prefer to sit in a corner.
5. You comment with others on each and every aspect which is happening around you.
6. When you are in a group, you laugh loudly.

7. Often you feel that you are not as handsome or as beautiful like him/her or you are not as tall as him/her, you are not as active as him/her.
8. You don't have a melodious voice, but whenever you get a chance, you try to sing songs.
9. Next day, you have to attend a meeting, meanwhile, whenever you find time, you rehearse in the bathroom and bedroom about how to talk in the meeting.
10. Whenever you talk to a person, you think how your words are influencing him/her without thinking what he/she is talking.
11. You have the same hobbies what everyone has, but never try to inculcate new hobbies.
12. Often your friends and family members tease you that sometimes when you speak with some particular people, you have a streak voice.
13. Whenever you find time, you boast about the greatness of your forefathers.
14. Whenever others compliment you, you feel very happy.
15. Your wife/husband or the people younger than you say that you speak like a boss.
16. In any gathering or party often, you display your defects by hitting the chair or dropping water upon you or slipping the spoon from your hand.
17. You daydream that you are above others.
18. You like to smoke a cigar or chew the gum, betel, or betel nut.
19. You can't keep quiet without boasting your achievements.
20. When you are losing an argument, you raise your voice.
21. When you sit among a group, you play with keychain, set the colour button or pull the hair string.
22. If you have to take a decision on an important thing, you feel very happy if your friends or relatives give some advice even if they don't have any knowledge regarding that aspect.
23. You feel jealous about many persons whom you know well.
24. Often you look into the eyes when you speak with others.

Persons with self-confidence never compare them with others. They analyse how 'best' they Performed and how 'best' they are Performing now!

Evaluation

In the above mentioned statements, if you get the answer, 'no' to the 1st & 24th, put one mark to each statement. Other than those two statements, if you get the answer, 'yes' to all of the questions, then put one mark to each statement.

If you score more marks or 15 and above marks, it shows that you have lots of inferiority complex.

If you score less marks, you are more confident!

What are the requirements of a person to improve self-confidence??

To know about yourself, to love yourself, to accept your limitations and use your plus points, etc.......

One thing you must always remember....

The people around you are interested only in your plus points, but not in your minus points. They are simply interested in what you can do and what you can give to them.

So don't sit around worrying about your weaknesses. Go ahead, think how best you can perform. Move forward with confidence that you can achieve what you want to achieve....

In order to improve your confidence levels, examine the following weaknesses in the lives of some great personalities.

- ❑ When Thomas Alva Edison went to school, within three months, his teacher remarked, "He has nothing in his brain. He can't do anything and he can't learn anything."
- ❑ In spite of his teacher's opinion, we all know how he proved his intellectualism. He invented the electric bulb, photography and the talkie movies...
- ❑ Albert Einstein was also like Edison and his teacher used to say that he could never learn maths in his life but he proved to be the one of the greatest mathematician of the 20th century.
- ❑ When Elvis Presley was in his eighth class, he wrote in his report card, "His chances of becoming a musician are nil." But Presley became a renowned singer and earned millions of dollars!
- ❑ Michelangelo and Socrates, both were ugly. Michelangelo with his beautiful paintings and Socrates with his philosophy stood immortal in the world history.
- ❑ English poets, Alexander Pope suffered numerous health problems and had a stunted growth. Byron suffered from a deformity of his right foot. Milton at the age of 44 became

completely blind, but produced great poems. These poets are considered as the greatest poets of the English literature.

- Somerset Maugham had a severe stutter. But the stutter never stood as an obstacle for him in achieving success as a story writer and novelist.
- Mozart was deaf but composed the best music and has remained as one of the most celebrated of all the composers.
- Chhatrapati Shivaji and Lal Bahadur Shastri were very short. In spite of their short stature, they became one of the greatest personalities and warriors of the world.

So even if there are drawbacks or some defects or deformities in your body, don't worry, just move ahead with confidence, and you'll achieve success. One of the well-known figures and the former American President, Roosevelt said:

"A person who doesn't do anything ever commits no mistakes!" Never fear of committing mistakes and faults. But take care of not repeating the mistakes and faults second time..."

Well then, if the above statements are true to life, then move to the next page-

Self-Confidence Tips

Confidence never comes by birth to any person. One can acquire it slowly through the experiences of life and by self-learning.

There is a close relationship between *self-confidence* and *success*. When a person achieves success, confidence increases. When confidence increases, it is easier to achieve success.

Self-confidence Helps to Achieve Success

The most important thing to remember regarding success is whenever a person beings a new work, he has a low confidence. After completion of that work, he feels confident in his mind that he can do it. It is natural! For example:

Suppose you are learning cycle riding or car driving. In the beginning, you ride or drive them with a fear. After perfect learning with full confidence and without any hesitation, you will easily ride the bicycle or drive the car.

As the skill increases, confidence shapes in a person! Even in other aspects of life, confidence works in the same manner. So in order to be, confident in the field (either a profession or any occupation) you are working, you should have complete understanding about that field, and should possess the complete skills and techniques.

Just like the above example, initially we have some doubts and fears in learning or beginning anything which is natural but there is no need of taking it seriously. As one's skill improves, fears vanish and with this thought one has to move ahead.

Any person moving ahead/forward by remembering his/her achievements and forgetting his/her failures can acquire self-confidence.

By remembering only the failures and not keeping the victories in mind, self-confidence dissolves in a person, and he eventually becomes nervous.

Remember Your Achievements

When your parents, without fulfilling your needs, or without giving the love and affection you need, nurture you carelessly, then the seed of insecurity builds in you. This feeling of insecurity makes you to lose self-confidence.

Good health helps you to shine in your profession and getting love and affection from your near and dear persons also makes you self-confident.

On the contrary, ill health, insults from others and despair and despondency repeating always in the life of a person, makes a person lose his/her self-confidence.

Whatever may be the reasons, a person who loses self-confidence in his/her life can regain it by following the below mentioned principles:

One Has to Learn to Impress Others

In order to shine in the society, we should be positive with our appearance. Our dressing and appearance should impress others. At the same time, the dressing should be comfortable and suitable for us.

A person in order to be always confident has to be in neat dressing.

One has to be seen neat not only when he attends an interview or meets important people or in special occasions, but also he has to be seen neat during his stay at home!

A person who feels 'special' in every moment of his/her life will always want to look neat Basically. One who wants to be neat beautiful or handsome always has a high confidence level.

The persons who have self-confidence have great 'love' for their appearance and individuality!

So love yourself. Display attention and concern upon your appearance and individuality. By doing so, you can boost your self-confidence!

Be Fit and Healthy

When the body is physically fit, energetic and strong, it will influence self-confidence. So by being fit and healthy, you are helping yourself.

We can be fit by participating in games or by doing exercises or of course, 'yoga'. There are many options. Play Tennis, go for Swimming or Jogging. If there is a 'Gym' nearby, join it and do exercises regularly.

Exercises make you feel fresh. The endorphin hormones released in the body makes the mind and the body relaxed. These hormones keep you in good mood and make you to work actively. All these aspects together are responsible to develop your self-confidence.

Imagine Yourself in a High Position

One of the important aspects to develop self-confidence is to understand yourself and to accept yourself!

Understand your defects and try to accept them. Nobody is perfect in this world. Everybody has his or her own set of defects or drawbacks.

So also, you have your own set of defects. First, accept them and try to correct them. By doing so, you can enable 'Healthy optimistic views'.

Share your feelings with others! Communication always helps to improve confidence.

Identify your dream or goal that gives happiness in your life and try to achieve it.

Self-confidence flourishes in us when we lead our lives happily and contented.

Self-confidence doubles in us when we appreciate ourselves, praise ourselves and treat ourselves as VIPs!

Keep a Safe Distance from Foxes

Each of us have friends as well as enemies in this world. It is easier to identify the visible enemies and we can be careful of them, but the enemies in the guise of friends and well-wishers are difficult to identify. We can call them as '**Foxes**'!

These foxes are in the guise of friends or relatives. They can be even in the guise of wife/husband. At times, they may not tolerate each other's progress. The progress can be in any aspect, such as that of education or occupation, wealth, happiness, etc.

When we are in a good mood, some of our so-called friends or relatives often spoil our moods by blaming us. They try to make us sad. By doing so, they want to kill the self-confidence in us.

We can identify those types of persons like this-

Every time when you feel sad, depressed and are full of sorrows, if you talk to a person, then you can make out that he/she is an above mentioned person (fox)!

These people or the so-called foxes behave in such a manner because they can't tolerate other person's progress and growth.

If a wife/husband behaves with his/her partner like this, it means he/she wants to control his/her partner and keep him/her under his/her hold.

Everyone has to be careful with these types of persons (foxes) who try to weaken the self-confidence of others. One must always try to be away from them.

Don't Stop Your Work in the Middle

Margaret Mitchell's novel, Gone with the wind was rejected by publishers for 38 times before its publication. However, after its publication, it has become one of the most successful novels in the world.

The more you practise self-discipline
The more you gain confidence.
The more you believe in yourself and
on your capabilities.

So whenever you start a work, don't stop in the middle. Many of them lose confidence and stop their work in the middle. Such persons are labelled as 'unstable persons' in the society.

In order to complete a task without stopping in the middle, from the beginning itself, it has to be done with proper planning, steadily, and with discipline.

If you stop the work in the middle without completing it, then it is difficult for you to erase the remark that you are an 'unstable person'. You also miss your opportunities with an assumption that 'he/she can't complete it!' So even if you are an intellectual, or a very intelligent and qualified person, you should take care of avoiding this remark upon you.

This remark not only makes others to lose confidence on you, but also makes you to lose confidence upon yourself!

The persons who are habituated to stop their work in the middle without completing it to the end have to follow the following methods and regain confidence while they speak with others in their day to day life :

Speak quietly and peacefully. Don't stop until you complete the sentence. When others interfere in the middle, tell them, "Wait, let me complete!"

This makes you to display your power and others take you seriously. Through this, there is a chance of regaining confidence slowly.

You can do what others can do.
Even you can do it well
But you need that 'temper'.

Take Failures as Lessons

Many persons feel very sad, when they face failure, they lose confidence. This is bad. Failures teach lessons like a teacher.

Failure is like a signpost that shows the correct route. It cautions us to take the correct route.

If there is no failure in one's life, that person is like a dead man! Life without any challenge is very dull. There won't be any thrill. Life would become too boring. Don't forget that people who achieve success, walk on the stones of failures!

There are lots of differences between successful persons and ordinary persons to accept their failures and their attitude towards failures. Successful persons always learn new lessons from failures. In fact, they gain a new confidence from each of their failures.

When you are haunted with any problem or challenge, be confident that you can come out of it and move ahead with confidence.

Nobody is perfect in this world. Nobody can be confident always. So when you face a failure, don't get discouraged and rise or bounce back like a ball.

You have to try again and again! It reveals your confidence levels…

Confidence means having a strong mind to accept failures! Through confidence, you can acquire the courage to take risks.

A person can be called greedy, if a person wants success every time in whatever work he undertakes. Let the failures occur, as they are just like steps towards the right way or path. Through failures, learn new lessons but don't lose confidence.

Bring out Positive Thoughts

A person first has to throw away the negative thoughts in order to gain confidence. He has to gather all his positive thoughts. The following methods can help you.

Suppose you are a salesperson and want to sell an article, first of all explain the best qualities of that article! So also, when you are a salesperson, think about what best qualities are there in you.

If you can't analyse the qualities, tick the following list of words whichever is applicable to you. While ticking, be honest! You are buying yourself! So be honest while ticking, don't deceive yourself.

❑ Honest person	⇨	Holy person
❑ Always speaks Truth	⇨	Creative Person
❑ Gracious Person	⇨	Hard Working
❑ Careful Person	⇨	Curious to achieve something
❑ Romantic	⇨	Able to Converse Skilfully
❑ Faithful	⇨	Intelligent
❑ Respectful	⇨	Intellectual
❑ Ethical	⇨	Speaks Respectfully
❑ Persons with Soul	⇨	Disciplined
❑ Respects the Law	⇨	Thoughtful
❑ Courageous	⇨	Acceptable to all
❑ Selfless	⇨	Skilful
❑ Obedient		

After ticking the applicable words from the above mentioned list….Are you now able to realise your best qualities?

You can feel proud of these qualities. Isn't it ?

Throw away the Negative Thoughts

Now think of your bad qualities or drawbacks and defects…..

For some time, forget that you are a respectable person! If you are unable to recognise your drawbacks, think of the bad qualities and defects that you hate in others, may be, you will realise that you have the same drawbacks -

For every bad quality, on the other side, there has to be a good quality. So try to bring out the good qualities from the bad qualities- for example:

- ❑ If you are a 'Restless person', you are a creative and hard working person.
- ❑ If you are a 'Hopeless Person', you are careful, thoughtful and faithful person.
- ❑ If you are 'Irresponsible Person', you are jovial and a happier person.
- ❑ If you are an 'Impractical Person', you are sensitive, creative and artistic person.
- ❑ If you are a 'Furious Person', you are a respectable, honest and a person who abides by the laws and principles of the society.
- ❑ If you are an 'Unromantic Person', you are a very practical person.

- If you are a 'Merciless Person', you are an opportunist want to go ahead in your career or business at any cost with your hard work.
- If you are a 'Shy Person', you are sensitive, thoughtful and a creative person.
- If you are a 'Sensitive Person', you are respectable, selfless and helping natured...

Like this, try to remember the positive qualities along with the negative qualities and learn to respect yourself!

To Err is Human

Some persons always feel sad and repent for their mistakes and errors. They must consider

The fact that every man in this world commits mistakes sometime or the other. Nobody does the right things always. One should not forget that..... *To err is human!*

Those who want to progress has to face the challenges of life. They have to take the risks. Sometimes your decisions or judgements may be wrong. Your decisions may bring failures, the people who depend on you may feel sad, during these situations who should gather your courage and be strong.

The mistake or the fault shows your weakness. Never hesitate to accept your fault. Your acceptance shows your confidence.

Remember

Your acceptance shows your mental maturity. Learning lessons from the mistakes shows your intelligence. The person who never commits mistakes, who don't experiment, will lose many opportunities.

Always remember that the need to do mistakes will come only once or twice in your life!

Before every great achievement,

There are many efforts and many failures.

Nobody sees them or talk about them.

Never Hesitate to Say, 'Don't Know'

Never hesitate to say, 'don't know' when you don't know about a particular thing. However small it may be, or you may feel shy for not knowing such a simple thing, still when you say that you don't know about it shows your mental ability.

Nobody in this world knows everything. In the newspapers, we often come across the statements of the great intellectuals and persons who have reached to the highest position often saying, "Still I have to learn more".

The weak, the foolish, the unstable and the ignorant persons only feel that they know everything in this world and never use the phrase that they 'don't know'.

The stable, and those who have a great mental ability always say they don't know about a thing which they really do not know. One should feel proud to genuinely accept the truth!

Be Self-Centred

Try to be self-centred in your life. The persons who have a low self-esteem, andwho are guilty will be more selfless. These persons spend most of their time thinking about others and regretting their mistakes.

If you are regretting and feeling sad about your guilt, keep them aside and try to understand your desires, your ideals and what are your goals of life. Bring out your desires from the depths of your heart and try to fulfil them.

Never be Depressed or Demoralised

Are you thinking that your life is a failure? Are you feeling sad by thinking that you are unable to lead a life full of pride or honour??

Just think of the prominent people and the prominent things in your life! Your partner (wife/husband), friends, your health, your children, your interests, your likes, your acquired knowledge, your memories, etc...... if you can understand all these aspects you'll be surprised!

Some people feel tensed about their future, which seems to them uncertain and dark. These types of people have to try to assess what extreme harm and destruction can take place in their future life. Then they will be quite surprised to find the truth that nothing has happened, as they feared. Then they feel lighthearted and develop a spiritual power in them!

If any person wants to have self-confidence in his thoughts, self-confidence has to be seen in every walk of his life. It will be useful to follow the below mentioned exercises in day-to-day life to gain self-confidence.

Lifelong you have to be a student.
The more you learn
The more you gain confidence.

Always Sit in the Front Seat

Many persons are habituated to sit in the back rows when they attend assemblies, meetings, classes and conferences. This happens because they lack confidence. Sitting in the front rows increases confidence. So make it a habit of sitting in the front row. While making it a habit, you feel 'self-conscious' about others and feel shy initially, but later you can do with it.

Remember that the people who want to achieve success should be away from being self-conscious and shyness!

Eye to Eye Contact

Many people, because of shyness or lack of confidence are unable to maintain eye contact with the people whom they are speaking. Even if others try to make an eye contact, these people turn away their eyes. By doing this, you may give an impression to others that you are hiding something or fearing to tell something.

Making eye contact not only gains others' confidence upon you, but also increases your self-confidence.

Don't be Quiet, Speak up

When you are with other persons, it is good to speak rather than sitting quietly and listening to them. You'll lose your confidence when you are unable to speak because of shyness or fear.

When the situation demands, it is better to speak, instead of hesitating, "Can I speak or not?" You can speak on anything-for instance, ask a question, give an advice or pass a comment. When you talk to others, your confidence acts as a vitamin.

Walking Fast

Body movements reveal the mind of a person. Confidence is seen in the person who walks fast with long footprints and grandeur. Your confidence grows up when you walk 25% faster than your regular pace.

If you keep your shoulders properly aligned with the rest of the body, your head up and eyes looking straight ahead and walk with long footprints, you'll feel proud that the street belongs to you. If you make this a habit, after some time, you'll improve self-confidence.

Laugh Loudly

There is no use of a small grin. Whenever time permits, laugh loudly. Loud laughter removes your distress, sorrows, sufferings and fears. Confidence settles in you.

Even if you are in depression, when you laugh loudly, you'll feel happy. Slowly the confidence that you long for enters into you.

Take Care of your Body Language

Your Body Language reveals your self-confidence and your condifence towards others.

Your body should be seen relaxed by others. If there are sudden and fast movements in your body, you'll send signals to others that you are in some mental stress.

You have to keep your head straight without moving this side or that side.

Your eyesight should be straight without looking away.

Don't put your hands often on your face.

Don't stiffen your shoulders.

Keep your waist straight.

Like this.......

(You can learn more information from the 'Body Language' series written by me....)

To Be Brief.....

By inculcating the following qualities in you, you will feel fully confident, such as:

- ❑ You have to accept that you are a special person, you have a special place in this world and you have to perform some special tasks.
- ❑ Don't waste time. Through proper time management, have a control over the time.
- ❑ Stop depending upon others. Never think of the fears, sufferings and guilt. Instead, try to develop love, imagination, enthusiasm, sense of humour and skilful conversation.
- ❑ Regularly practise Meditation to gain peace of mind, enhance your capabilities and get satisfaction, ultimately gaining confidence.
- ❑ Always have a belief upon yourself. Never be doubtful upon your capabilities.
- ❑ Get mentally prepared that you have to face difficulties or sorrows and sufferings at any time or at any stage of your life.
- ❑ Feel the happiness and satisfaction in the work you are doing, so that you do not feel disappointed. If you are disappointed, you'll lose your confidence.

You are a 'New Person'

As mentioned above, if you have positive thoughts in your mind, you can work positively. Then you'll become a 'new person' with full confidence. The delightful 'new person' will be somewhat like this:

- You will never be lonely, but remain friendly with all the people.
- Your future will not be in the hands of others, but you can have a full control on it.
- You will always be decent and dignified.
- You will always be in a state of inviting new values, principles and beliefs.
- You will lead a long and healthy life.
- You will be able to love yourself more and also others.

So in this 'new person', are you able to see a great personality?

This is known as perfect confidence!!

"BE WHAT YOU WANT TO BE."

"Before trying to be a master of others, be sure, you are the master of yourself" –

– Napoleon Hill

Be Positive

You are standing under a tree, suddenly a huge bough falls beside you. It is so huge that if it would have fallen upon you, you might have died there itself.....

Immediately after the fall of the bough:

(A) You feel relieved and thank God for not making it to fall upon you, or

(B) You feel tensed by thinking that "what would have happened to me if it fell upon me?"

If your answer is (A), you are a man with positive thinking.

If your answer is (B), you are a man with negative thinking.

Positive thinking is a philosophy that makes your life go in a right direction. Positive thinking or a positive attitude makes you to control your life and enables you to solve the problems that you face in your life easily and quickly.

Positive thinking makes us to mould many situations according to us.

Positive thoughts help us to lead a serene life.

Serene life means to be happy, to be peaceful, to be healthy, to be successful, etc......

Generally, if a man faces many obstacles in his life, he feels and remains unhappy and starts thinking negatively.

If life goes happily, he thinks positively.

This is the basic equation for positive and negative thoughts.

Now, you may feel that thinking positively or negatively is not in your hands, so what can you do? The answer for this is:

There are many opportunities in life to think positively, even if there are many problems that one has to face in one's life, especially through an optimistic mind.

Through optimism, we can change our lifestyle. We can change our attitude, and through it we can bring positive thinking into our lives.

To be positive once in a day is not sufficient. In every aspect and in every situation, you have to think positively. Then only positive thinking absorbs into your nerves! Absorbs into your subconscious!!

When you think positively, often consciously or unconsciously that will absorb into your subconscious mind, and through it you can mould your life according to your decisions.

Conscious,

Subconscious......

The actions and thoughts that we make which are known to our mind belong to the category of consciousness, whereas the actions and thoughts that we make unconsciously belong to the category of subconsciousness.

If we want to separate our mind into two parts, one is the conscious mind and the other is the subconscious mind.

The day to day situations and the decisions that are taken logically and rationally occurs through the conscious mind. Not the habituated situations, but the decisions taken in the new situations.

For example, you are learning to drive a car or a scooter. During the initial period and until few months, you think consciously and change the gears and brakes. While changing gears and brakes, you think consciously and take decisions consciously.

Without your knowledge, the unconscious decisions and actions are done through the subconscious mind. The habitual actions after doing them over and over again are related to the subconscious mind.

Let's take the above-mentioned example of car driving. After learning to drive perfectly, whenever you drive, according to the situation unknowingly and unconsciously, you change the gears and brakes. During that time, you may be thinking of your office and what to do there or planning to collect the money from your friend,who has taken a loan from you long back, etc.

Even with these thoughts, the actions you make (i.e., here changing the gears and the brakes) unconsciously will conduct your subconscious mind.

The same happens with positive thinking as well. If you try to make the habit of thinking positively in every matter, slowly these thoughts will absorb into your mind. It is very important for every person to have positive thoughts.

Positive thoughts help to achieve success in life. They will build confidence in you. You can think high about yourself. They also help to shape your personality in a positive way.

The Negative Perspective:

If you think that you are a failure, you will get negative thoughts and will face failures only. Instead, if you think that you are an able competitor, you can come out any problem easily..

"I am fit for nothing",

If you think that you are fit for nothing and you can't do anything, you will really become a negative person and be unable to do anything successfully in your life.

To be positive means worrying less and enjoying more, forgetting sad things and remembering happy occasions. Leaving unhappiness and choosing happiness!

The first step towards positive thinking is to be positive about yourself! Feel good about yourself! If you are positive with your own self, others will also respond to you positively.

Don't feel very sad or upset when any tragedy or misfortune takes place in your life. Don't develop grudge upon the persons who are responsible for the misfortune. If you are responsible for that don't regret.

These are the aspects of negative thinking .....

The difference between a positive thinking person and a negative thinking person:

When there is a problem, the positive thinking person takes it as a challenge. With self-confidence, he tries to solve it.

A negative thinking person tries to run away from the problem with the fear that he can't face the problem and makes the situation even worse.

To be Positive..........

To be positive, follow the methods mentioned below:

- ❑ Be friendly with the people around you. Try to help them. Talk to them whole-heartedly, but don't be like a doormat.
- ❑ Find out your needs and try to achieve them. Don't be greedy, you should not deceive others to achieve your needs.
- ❑ You should be optimistic and this optimism should be a realistic one.

- ❑ Be selfish to some extent but your selfishness should not affect others' opportunities. Your selfishness should not bring any loss to others.

Basically, to have a positive thinking, try to inculcate the following habits into your lifestyle:

Control your Moods

- ❑ In any incident that occurs in your life, you are responsible for your behaviour and feelings. First, you have to accept it. You can't control the incidents that happen in your life or control the behaviour and actions of others, but you can control your actions or behaviour.
- ❑ Regarding such situations, the way you respond, the way you feel are in your hands isn't it?! Control your feelings and see that they are positive ones. For example :
- ❑ Your boss says something about you in the office. You come home with a lot of stress. In that mood, misbehave or scoldyour wife and children unnecessarily. It results in an unhappy situation and disturbs your family atmosphere .... Whose is responsible for it? Your boss or yourself? Who are the sufferers, your boss or yourself??
- ❑ You can't control your boss's actions or behaviour, but you can certainly control your actions or behaviour and the way you respond to your boss's behaviour
- ❑ Supposing your boss is foolish, and can't control his family tensions – letting them out on his/her subordinates at the office doesn't mean that you let out your frustrations on your family members at home. This seems ridiculous.
- ❑ The only solution to the problem is donot take his words to heart and donot carry your office at home. Thre should be p[roper distinction and partition between office and home.
- ❑ Basically, if you concentrate on the happier things of life ignoring the sad things,, there will be no question of disappointments, ill-feelings or bad mood.

So, without trying to control the behaviour of others, if you try to control your mind and your moods, you'll shape yourself as a perfect gentleman.

Everything is for Good

If any incident happens in your life, accept it with a philosophical note that 'everything happens for good'.

Don't sit wailing or brooding if any misfortune occurs or tragedy takes place or you face any kind of injustice. You may gain fortune from your misfortune, you may gain compassion or such experiences may teach you a lesson in your life.....

If you think like this, you can react positively.

Failure is in Your Mind

When you start a work and face failure in it don't be disappointed. Think that it is just a small blow in the path of achieving success.

Your journey never stops with it. It is a halting place in a journey.

Take the failure as a guideline, see that it is not repeated again, and move forward to achieve success. So never, allow failures to get into your mind, but take it as a lesson.

Don't be Idle without Work

- ❑ Never sit idle. If you are free by any reason, select any of your favourite work (it can be your hobby) and get completely absorbed in it.
- ❑ An idle man's mind is a devil's workshop, so never be idle because then all negative thoughts will surround your mind.
- ❑ Always engage your mind with some creative work.

Help Others

- ❑ Try to help persons whom you know or people who seek your help in their sorrows or troubles. By helping them, you can find a solution to those troubles when you face them. This will help you in your later life.
- ❑ For example, your neighbour has a heart attack at midnight. By helping him that night, you can learn what to do and how to react in such an emergency. Your neighbours also show gratitude for your help....

Say, 'Sorry' Whenever Required

- ❑ Because of any reason, knowingly or unknowingly, if you have created a problem or trouble in anybody's mind, never hesitate to say, 'sorry'. You can also ask an apology for your mistake. There is nothing to feel low about it.

- Try to explain them in what conditions you have reacted like that, and if you do so, he/she will change the negative feelings on you.

Don't Show Self-Pity

- Self-pity destroys a person. If you keep pitying yourself, life will become dull and you may not be able to work properly.
- Remember, you alone can help yourself. If you start pitying yourself, you will stay there without development.
- So leave self-pity upon yourself and concentrate on your work. In this regard, nobody will help you, but you, yourself.

Don't Take Advices from Everybody

- There are many people to give you free advice. If you ask for a person's advice, he will feel that he is greater or wiser than you. This is an aspect of satisfying one's ego! So don't take advice from whoever you meet.
- Only take advice from the experienced or elderly persons, who are able to give advice and are eligible to give advice.
- There is a danger of getting misguided if you take advice from all. It may not be all that good.

Don't Try to Control Others

- Many people have a bad quality. They always want to control others and want them to do things according to their will.
- This shows their wicked and dominating nature. One day it will bring harm to themselves with such type of attitude. So be careful and avoid such kind of people in the society.
- If you have a very dominating or controlling nature, get rid of it immediately, or the best way is to control yourself. This helps you a lot. Some foolish wives and husbands who are of such type are the best examples and they ruin their respective family lives by doing so.

Invite Friendly Criticisms

- If your well-wishers and friends make any remark or comment on you, don't react negatively. Try to analyse the merits and demerits in it.

- This will help you to know how others think about you. You will know about your shortcomings/drawbacks and the things you have to set right. This will give you a fair chance to rectify them.

So don't be afraid or feel embarrassed by friendly remarks and criticisms. Encourage these types of remarks and take them positively to improve yourself. Then only you can live with a positive attitude in the society.

"Your reputation is what people think you are, your character is what you are." – Napoleon Hill

A Successful Boss

Helen Gurley Brown who has started a large number of editions worldwide and retired as an editorial director for the English News paper 'Cosmopolitan' has revealed her success secrets in the following manner:

- Say "No" to the persons who waste their time with unnecessary talk.
- Try to work hard than others, make it a habit
- First do the less pleasant tasks later do the happier and pleasant tasks
- Before criticising your subordinates speak one or two good words about them
- While speaking with the subordinates give complete credit to them. But when you speak with your Boss speak less
- Before shouting at others check yourself that you are shouting at them with right reason
- When you make a mistake be ready to accept it.
- Don't lose your patience, it will show that you are not having control on yourself

Be Away from Negative Feelings...

(You are responsible for yourself)

You may be a sixteen-year-old teenager, twenty-five years old young man, a forty years old middle-aged man, or a sixty years old man. You may be struggling with your studies or wandering for a job.

You may earn lots of money with a stable job or you may be having vicissitudes with your business.

You may be suffering from different kinds of problems or living a comfortable, happy and contented life.

'Whoever' you may be, or in 'whatever' situation you may be, you have to accept the truth that you are responsible for the life you live, for your position in the society and your present condition.

Your thinking, your lifestyle, the way you face the failures and successes, handling of your emotions, your determination, your efforts or lack of all these qualities in you, will influence your life positively or negatively. All the above factors are responsible for your present condition, whether you accept it or not, this is the reality!!

If you dislike your lifestyle and present conditions, if you want them to change, first change yourself without waiting for the society around you to change!

Change Your Way of Thinking

Your way of thinking influences your attitude and behaviour and it will affect your failures and successes in your life. **In one word, failures and successes of your life depend upon the way you think.**

We all have a bad quality. We wait for somebody to come and set right our lives which is absurd. From our childhood, our minds have been tuned up with the thought that some person/persons is/are responsible for our lives..Basically, parents are responsible for inducing this type of thought because they generally fulfil all our needs from our childhood!

From our childhood to adolescence, parents provide us food, dress, education, etc and look after us without any insufficiency. They give us money for our luxuries, when we are ill, they take care of us and spend money for our treatment. It continues like this until we reach our adolescence and this type of treatment unconsciously imprints on our mind that somebody is responsible (here parents) to lead our lives. After adolescence, it means from 18 to 20, one has to lead a lonely life.

It means till adolescence, somebody has driven your lives and from adolescence, you have to sit in the driving seat and take complete charge of your life as you have grown up into an adult.

From then onwards, you begin to mould your life, and in fact, write your own destiny. You have to learn to solve your own problems....

But the way you were brought up from your childhood makes you think that somebody will fulfil your needs and they have to, and this expectation lingers in the mind unconsciously.

You're the 'Creator' of Your Life

Who are you? What do you want to become depends upon your thoughts, decisions and the things you do. So you are the 'creator' of your life, you'll write your own future. This will influence your lifestyle, attitude and quality of life. You should be careful about your thoughts from your adolescence! You have to adopt self-responsibility.

The person one who takes self-responsibility achieves perfect maturity.

So many people boast about themselves when they achieve success and blame others and 'bad luck' when they face failures.

But the people who adopt self- responsibility are not like that. They will take responsibility for all the failures and successes faced in their lives.

Taking Responsibility at Workplace

The employees in big companies who are in the top positions (these people constitute about 3% of any company) say that it is their own company. Whenever they speak of their job, they say that they are self-employed. When they talk about the company, they say "my company", "my factory", etc. But the ordinary employee in that company is not like that. He feels that he is separate and the company is separate. He speaks as if he has no recognition in it.

If you work in a company or in an organisation with a feeling, that it is your own company, your company will prosper as well as you can prosper. In other words, if you want to reach a high position in any job or company, or you want the company to prosper, you have to feel or take the responsibilities! You should feel that it is your own company.

Your earnings, financial status, your position in the society, your designation/level, your recognition, everything depends upon the degree of responsibility felt or taken by you.

For example –

Suppose you are the owner of a company. There is a vacancy for a post. So you want to select one out of the two subordinate staff. One person out of the two works day and night for the company as if it is his own and the other person works as an employee, i.e., comes at 9 a.m and goes at 5 p.m.

For whom you'll give the promotion?

For whom do you want to give a rise in the salary??

For whom you'll arrange additional training ???

Definitely for the first person .... Isn't it ??

Being honest and feeling responsible in the job are the two important aspects of success.

What and Who are You?

When you self-examine yourself that what you are and what sort of person you are, first self -examine yourself that what is your attitude towards self-responsibility.

Taking the responsibility completely or not taking any responsibility- you will be somewhere in this scale.

The person who yields towards not taking any responsibility in the scale will have negative thoughts. He is a pessimist, often faces failures, fearful, no goals in life, neurotic, etc.

The person who yields towards taking complete responsibility in the scale will have positive attitude, self-confidence, and can control himself in any situation, and possess a healthy mind.

When you are able to take the responsibility in any aspect of the life then you can have control on yourself. When you are able to control yourself, you'll feel free and happy.

In other words-

The more you feel responsible the more you can have a control over yourself and the situation you are in. You'll feel free. All these aspects increase positive thoughts.

So also-

If you lack self-responsibility, you'll lose control upon yourself, lose your freedom, and then the negative thoughts will increase and surround your mind and thoughts..

Negative Emotions

Negative thoughts and motions will not allow you to achieve anything in your life and can make you face failures.

A person has to achieve peace of mind first! If he struggles with negative emotions, he will never have peace of mind in his life.

You should be either with peace of mind or with negative emotions. Your mind can't withstand both these emotions together.

When you let out your negative emotions, your life will be wonderful and happier.Even if you do attain success, your achievement will not give you happiness but can lead to health disorders like ulcers, blood pressure problems and other cardiac ailments.

So in order to achieve Pleasure, Happiness, Liberty and Prosperity in life, first let out your negative emotions and negative thoughts from your mind.

Many times, we feel that it is natural for negative emotions to arise in our minds. But it's not correct. Negative emotions do not occur in a person by birth. **Have you ever observed negative emotions in infants?? Never, as it is almost impossible!!**

As we, adults adopt and experience negative emotions from our childhood through imitation, practice and through learning, so we can come out and get rid of them also and feel free.

What are Negative Emotions?

The negative emotions that are common in everybody and that can be easily recognised are:

❑ Disbelief	❑ Guilt
❑ Fear	❑ Jealousy

It is acknowledged that there are about fifty and above negative emotions in a person. When all these emotions are combined, the important emotion that comes out is anger!

Characteristics of Anger

The most powerful and destructive negative emotion is anger! When anger enters into a person, his blood boils and he shouts at others. If he suppresses anger in himself, he is prone to diseases or if he shows it on others, he has to lose relationships. So in any way anger does no good.....

Think once,

- How are your feelings when you are in anger?
- Are you able to think in the right manner?
- Can you adjust with others?
- Can you sleep well?
- Does the food you take is digested properly?
- When you are in anger, do you feel gloomy?
- Do you have concentration?
- Are you able to think of other aspects when you are in an angry mood?
- Do you repeatedly think of the injustice and mutter about it?

So as long as you continue in an angry mood, you can't have any sleep or peace of mind and you behave desolately. Either anger or negative emotions do no 'good' to you.

Now let us try to understand how negative emotions are shaped in our minds:

Reasons for Negative Emotions

There are four reasons to shape up the negative emotions in a person:

- **When you want to defend yourself**: It is natural to get angry when a person faces injustice or when others try to take advantage of him. The person also feels that it is his right to get anger....
  In those situations, he or she will search for people to be on his/her side and try to share his/her emotions. He/She tries to justify his/her anger. If he or she doesn't do this, his/her anger doesn't last longer!
  When a man is able to think that he is also responsible for the anger that comes out of him, then his anger cools down immediately, or even when he excuses the person who caused him this harm, there won't be any chance for anger.
- **When you examine everything in your point of view**: It is natural to get angry for trivial aspects when you view everything in your point of view.

Suppose, when there is an argument between a person and you in a particular situation, and you think that you are correct without ever trying to understand the other person's point is called as examining everything in your point of view. However,when you try to imagine yourself in other person's position and try to understand his point of view, definitely you will show compassion towards him. Then even if he/she is wrong, you may not show your anger upon him.

When you feel that you are ignored: It is quite natural to get angry when you notice others ignoring you. When you are among others and a person insults you, your 'Ego' hurts and as a result, you get angry. But one thing is there that others may not remember that incident as you remember, so try to forget it as soon as possible.

- **When you throw the blame upon others**: You'll try to throw the blame on others for your negative emotions. Around 99 percent of the people do so. Mostly negative emotions form in you because you think that others are responsible for your unhappiness. When you keep this thought aside and try to think that you are also responsible for your unhappiness then you can come out of the negative emotions.

Both positive and negative thoughts never go together in your mind. So when you are with negative thoughts, forcefully bring the positive thoughts into your mind and then automatically, you will be free from negative thoughts. For that you need concentration and will power.

Positive thoughts act as a foundation and give health, happiness, success and long life to a person, whereas, negative thoughts cause destruction in a person.

So every person has to make it mandatory to put down the negative thoughts from one's mind.

Positive Thoughts

- Hoping that everything will be good in future.
- Confidently thinking that you will definitely achieve what you want to achieve
- Remembering the happiest incidents of the past
- Confidence in people
- Eager to help others
- Feeling content for every trivial result
- Self-confidence and self-love

- Smile happily
- Enjoy the life
- To be content with what you have

Etc… all these aspects help you to achieve success in your life.

How are Negative Emotions Formed?

A person acquires negative emotions through his family and the members of his family. In his childhood, he develops them from his mother or father. According to the attitudes and the mindset of his parents, he too will identify himself with them and develop the same feelings. The same goes in the case of girls.

Another two experiences that inspire negative emotions from your childhood are:

1. Negative remarks from parents
2. Lovelessness

Negative Remarks from Parents: Children until they reach six years depend on their parents or others, who nurture them. They are also greatly influenced by their parents. So they believe in whatever their parents tell them. Parents also should be careful while nurturing them and giving their love to them.

By any reason, parents should not scold their children by saying, "You can't do anything," "you are a useless fellow," "you are an unfortunate fellow", etc. These negative remarks make the child emotionally upset. Fear and anxiety takes place in his mind. From then onwards, gradually he begins to respond to everything and becomes sensitive. In his later life also, he will responds quickly and be very reactive to every trivial incident and get angry. It could also be as a defensive reaction on his wife or boss or friend or colleague,when they say no to him.

Such sort of persons suffer lifelong from negative emotions like disbelief, fear and anger. So they have to do the following to overcome their negative feelings:

Whenever they feel that they are hurt, these types of persons can think from other person's point of view, and by doing so, they can be away from negative emotions.

- **Lovelessness**: If a child does not get love from the parents, he will be upset, cranky, moody, insecure and worried. Lovelessness should be in particular situations or on particular days, but when it is a continuous process, the child's heart begins to 'wither'.

Later it leads to many personality disorders. Gradually, he develops anger upon the world and develops a negative feeling or thinking towards the world.

In order to give complete love and affection to a child, parents should possess the following three qualities mentioned below:

- ❑ Both the parents should love themselves and possess self-esteem! If they don't love themselves, they can't give love to their children.
- ❑ The child watches, observes and experiences the love between the mother and the father, develops a secured feeling and self-confidence which deepens in his nature.
- ❑ As a result without any negative emotions, he/she can achieve victory in every task.

So parents should love their children. When the above said two points are followed by the parents, automatically the third point will take place.

Forgiving Nature

Negative feelings are formed when others do harm to you. So if you forgive them immediately, you can come out of the negative feelings. The other person may be wicked, senseless and cruel, still if you can forgive him/her, you can be free from negative feelings, or else, you will be destroying your own happiness.

By forgiving, you are doing good to yourself. Because you'll have peace of mind and peace of mind is one of the most important factors in bringing success through happiness. So never hesitate to forgive.....

Negative Thoughts

- ❑ Worrying about future
- ❑ Thinking that you are fit for nothing
- ❑ Recollecting the sad and sorrowful situations of the past
- ❑ Thinking that someone will harm you or you want to harm someone
- ❑ Not trusting people
- ❑ Fear regarding failures. Thinking that if anything is done, it may fail.
- ❑ Feeling lonely
- ❑ Repenting for the faults
- ❑ Vengeance
- ❑ Weeping for the departed souls (loved ones/lover or beloved)
- ❑ Jealousy

All these thoughts stand as barriers and do not allow you to achieve success.

Practise

To attain a forgiving nature, you have to do an exercise:

Whenever you are free, with a peace mind take a paper, and write down the names of the people who you think that they have done some harm to you. In front of each name, write down the harm he/she did to you. Now read the paper from top to bottom. When you read each name also recollect the harm they did.

After recollecting their harm done to you now in your mind start saying, "I'm forgiving his/her harm and never shall I think about it." Say it three to four times, likewise say about each name.

Now keep the paper aside. Whenever you recollect those people, who did harm to you again take away that negative emotion by saying, "I have forgiven him completely, so there is no need of thinking over it again and again.".

So in order to open the door of 'peace' in mind, the key of 'forgiving' will be a useful tool.

Self-examination

Suppose you made a wrong or did a harm to others because of any reason, immediately go to him/her and say, "I'm very sorry for the thing that happened."

By saying so you'll be out of the guilty feeling and again, you can regain your self-esteem.

Don't think about the person to whom you said, 'sorry' regarding how he reacts or how he feels. By saying sorry, you are accepting your guilt or fault and taking the responsibility for your actions. This shows your confidence and your character. This is important !! So feel proud about it……

"BE WHAT YOU WANT TO BE."

"Life is like a horse. If you can't ride the life, life will ride on you. Do you want to be a 'horse' or to be a 'rider' - everything depends upon the way you think."

Will-Power

Your outward life is interrelated to your psychological life. According to your thoughts, you will face the situations.

When we read the life histories of the people who excelled in different fields, won the name and fame, we can notice one common quality, that is:

In order to reach their goals, they had the will to move ahead with a strong determination and self-confidence even when they had to face obstacles and hardships.

To reach one's goal, every person should believe in himself or herself. When he or she faces any obstacles, impediments and failures, instead of worrying, he/she should react intelligently and take care that mistakes do not happen again and again.

To behave in the above mentioned manner, a person needs "will power".

What is 'willpower'??

To know about willpower, first one has to know about the 'mind'.

Two Minds

Every person has two minds:

- One – *The conscious mind*
- Second – *The subconscious mind*

We can exemplify these two minds like this-

Imagine two joined balls

- One – golf ball
- Second – basketball

Imagine on the above part, there is a golf ball and on the part below, it is the basketball.

Now the golf ball is your conscious mind and the basketball is your subconscious or the unconscious mind.

These two minds perform different actions, but both are interrelated. Both depend on one another.

In today's computer language, we can say that-

Conscious mind is the programmer. It works as a *computer operator* collecting all the outside information according to our thoughts and sends the needed data to the brain, which acts as a *computer.*

The subconscious mind is like the *computer hardware.* In its frame the *data,* which is sent by the conscious mind, will operate.

Your understanding about yourself or your self-concept works in your brain as a computer software programme and decides the result you achieve in your life.

Every experience and its result in your life depends upon how skilfully you are able to understand and use your conscious and subconscious mind.

When you are able to coordinate your conscious mind with the subconscious mind, then you can achieve success very fast and in a lesser time.

Now let's look about each type of mind.......

Do you want to be a 'different person'?

Write on a paper about how you want to be a 'different person'.

Now think that how you can fill the gap between you and the 'different person'.

Think about three persons who are leading their lives as you want to lead your life.

Try to move closer with them and learn lessons through their experiences.

Conscious Mind

'Victorious' – feels relaxed
mentally and physically
even in stressful situations
The quality to be 'cool' is not
acquired by birth but only
through learning!

The thoughts you make are with the conscious mind, and there won't be any memory in it. The conscious mind can make only one thought at one time.

Our Conscious Mind Can Make Four Things:

- **The First thing**, it identifies the message that come into our minds. It also identifies the messages through our sense organs-vision, sound, smell, taste and sense. Your conscious observes everything that happens around you.
  For example, when you are walking on the road and want to cross it suddenly, you'll listen to a car horn, stop there, and look at it.
  You'll look to know, 'what sound it is' and 'from how far it is coming'.
  This is the first activity done by your conscious mind.
- The **Second thing** done by your conscious mind is comparison! All the information regarding the car will reach your subconscious mind and this information can be compared with all the experiences and information that are already stored in the subconscious mind.
  For example: If the car is two hundred yards away and is running with a speed of 20 to 30 kms, your subconscious mind with its memory bank signals you that there is no danger with the car even when you cross it.
  If not, when the car is one hundred yards away and is running with a speed of 50 to 60 kms it gives you the signal of the 'danger' and stimulates you what to do next.
- The **Third thing** done by your conscious mind is 'analysis'.
- The **Fourth thing** is 'choice making'
  While making the choice, your conscious mind takes two types of freedom. It can accept or reject the information that is coming from outside.
  The conscious mind can make only one thought at one time. It may be a positive thought or a negative thought, but it cannot be both the thoughts at a time.

(If you are interested to know more about the conscious mind and the subconscious mind, read '**Body Psychology**' written by me.)

According to the mathematics scientist, Peter Ouspensky, our subconscious mind works thirty thousand times faster than our conscious mind!

In order to make your life brighter, know the power of your subconscious mind, understand how to activate it and use it.

This is what **will-power** means!

To understand this, first you have to know what the subconscious mind is and how it works in detail.

Subconscious Mind

The subconscious mind is like a big 'memory bank'. Its capacity is unlimited. All the incidents that occur in our lives are installed forever.

When a person reaches twenty- one years, his subconscious mind stores information hundred times more than Britannica encyclopedia information.

The subconscious mind never takes independent decisions but accepts the commands of the conscious mind and implements them. The conscious mind is like a gardener and the subconscious mind is like a garden or fertile soil. Whatever seeds the gardener sows, those types of plants will be grown.

So also according to the thoughts of your conscious mind, you can see the results of your subconscious mind.

According to your thoughts, principles and desires filled with emotions, your subconscious works as a servant day in and day out.

So in the life of garden, the subconscious mind can breed flowers or weeds. The result depends upon the seeds sown by your conscious mind.

The Work of a Subconscious Mind

The subconscious mind silently accepts every feeling and every thought made by the conscious mind. It tries to regulate the aspects that you see, and listen and notice from the surroundings. It means the subconscious mind will make you to see, to listen and to observe the things that are important for you (your conscious mind).

Particularly,when you feel more emotional about certain things -- those are very important, and your subconscious mind will alert you regarding those things and encourages you to achieve them in reality.

When you want to achieve a result, you have implant that desire deeply into your subconscious mind. That desire should reach like a command into your subconscious mind.

When the subconscious mind accepts the command, it motivates your thoughts and deeds to fulfil your desire. It also slowly builds up confidence in you and makes you a 'Better Person'.

As You Sow, So Shall You Reap

It is very difficult to achieve success in a work, if you can't devote time and energy towards it. Without thinking about the work to be achieved, if you think differently, the result will be nil.

The persons who want to achieve success will think about what they want to do and talk about the related things by building up self-discipline.

They will suppress their minds and not think of the unimportant things and unwanted matter. These persons will achieve extraordinary things, while other persons struggle with their routine work.

Concentration

Instead of starting four or five tasks at a time and unable to complete anyone, it is better to do the most important task with all your heart and mind without any fears and doubts. If you follow this, you can complete that task even if it takes time. This is what '**concentration**' means!

When you are able to control yourself, your mind will be always peaceful and you can also achieve the things that you want to achieve. This is the secret of people who want to achieve success and happiness-

Never think of your 'problem'

Never talk of your 'problem'

Talk about the 'solution'

Think about the 'solution'

Concentrate your mind on how to move forward in the future. Never think of what happened in the past....

Thinking about the solution is a positive attitude. Instead of thinking what happened, why did it happen, etc., if you think to find a solution to the problem, then your mind would be clear. You can solve the problem easily and quickly!

All are equal before the God of Success

Never forget that like others,

you are also entitled to achieve

success and happiness.

Never doubt about your self-worth.

By nature and opportunities, there can be differences between you and the others regarding success and happiness, but you, too are also eligible for success and happiness!

Sometimes, when things go wrong and when you are depressed, if you think like this- "I like myself. I like my attitude and profession" then all such feelings of sadness are neutralised.

Not once, but think like this repeatedly, and by doing so, you can also improve your self-esteem and your self-concept. Whenever you utter this statement, your subconscious mind takes it as a command and encourages you to love yourself. With this, even if you have any negative thoughts in your mind regarding your self-esteem, slowly they are erased from your mind.

That's why sometimes you have to feel –"I like myself"- as it is very important to think like this!

Learn like a game, to take the 'positive' aspect from every situation. About 95% of your anger depends upon the way how you look at a situation!

An Old Story

Long ago in Greece, a traveller asked an old man, "How to reach Mount Olympus?" The old man was Socrates! Socrates replied, "If you really want to reach Mount Olympus, make sure that every step has to go in the same direction!" When we apply this statement to our life we can say that:

To achieve success and happiness in our lives, every thought and every action of ours has to lead us towards that goal!

Sir Isaac Newton, an English physicist and mathematician, who was the culminating figure of the scientific revolution of the 17th century, with discoveries in optics, motion, and mathematics, developed the principles of modern physics. It was one of the most important single work in the history of modern science. In his last days, a person asked him:

"How can you alone initiate all these great things in science?"

Sir Isaac Newton replied like this: "I never thought of other things!"

Same with the case of success- You have to control the thoughts of your conscious mind. Always you have to concentrate on the goal you have chosen. For this, you have to follow a mental discipline. You have to display a great will power too.

Some people lead their lives as though they are walking in their sleep. They make unnecessary thoughts and spend their lives busily. These types of people should wake up from such a kind of life.

Our thoughts and our lives should not be mechanical. We have to regain our will power and control our thoughts and our lives according to our wishes.

*For this, you have to lead your life with more prudence, vigilance and awareness, so you have to control your thoughts.*You have to sit before the steering wheel of your life and drive it without giving the steering wheel to others.

You Can Do It

To display sufficient will power to tackle any situation, you need a lot of patience, peace of mind and self-confidence!

To achieve anything, your mind should be ready with sufficient will power, and then you will not have to wander for the thing you want, but it will come towards you automatically. Your determination paves the way for it, and for this, you need a clear understanding about what you want and what is your goal.

(For more information, you can read this in my other book,'**Time Management**')

Yes You Can

To display will power in your life, you have to follow some exercises. One is-

Take a white paper and write down all the things that you desire in your life.

Happiness, health, good friends, travel, development, money earning, name and fame, recognition, respect from others......etc. Write down all the desires that come into your imagination.....

For the next twenty-four hours, try to think about the points that you have written in the list and. never think about other things or talk about other things.

If you spend the whole day without criticising or worrying about the other things or without getting angry on anything and only concentrating on the list of points, then it shows you have will power.

This is very difficult to do because while performing the daily chores and conversing with others, one has to perform this exercise.

If you are able to perform this exercise, then you can acquire the will power, or else, read this chapter again, especially regarding the conscious mind and the subconscious mind and their functions....

> *"The two kinds of people who never get ahead are those who do only what they are told and those who do not do what they are told."* – W. Clement Stove

To Control Emotions – Self-discipline is a Must

Many of us think about the results after doing a work, but self-disciplined persons are not like that. They think about the pros and cons. To exhibit self-discipline, you have to control your emotions.

Following are the positive and negative emotions of a person:

Positive Emotions	Negative Emotions
love	fear
sex	jealousy

Positive Emotions	Negative Emotions
desire	hatred
belief	vengeance
enthusiasm	greed
confidence	anger
desire	superstition

We can control all the above emotions with some efforts. So controlling the emotions is self-discipline.

Balancing our emotions through reasoning is called self-discipline. It means, before taking a decision, we have to consult not only our feelings, but also our reasoning!

Sometimes, we have to keep aside our emotions and go according to the reason and sometimes we have to go according to our emotions. In those situations, you have to choose the way that gives you happiness, that doesn't harm you and gives you success.

Remember, your emotions never harm you. They are the driving force behind all your decisions.

Emotions are like river water, with obstruction and controlled usage one can be benefitted, but its overflow may result in severe problems.

Negative emotions are also controlled in the same manner through self-discipline and positive mental attitude and one can prevent the negative consequences by using them constructively.

Do you know the power that provides balance between emotions and reason?

Your will-power! Do you know the creative power that provides your will power??

Self-discipline!

Self-discipline

Any person in order to achieve success has to utilise his complete powers. To display the capabilities, he or she should possess self-discipline in his thoughts. This is an important factor in achieving success.

According to an observation, about 5% of the people in the society are utilising their maximum capabilities. Only these 5% even after their retirement stand on their own feet without depending financially upon others.

Do you want to be one among the 95%, or to be one among the above, 5%?

If you want to be in 5%, then you have to learn to exhibit self-discipline.

If a person wants to become a doctor, he has to study medicine and practise it. If he wants to become an engineer, he has to study engineering and undergo training under experts. If he wants to become a chef, he has to study cookery books and learn cooking. Isn't it ?? So also to achieve success, one has to know how to achieve it and study the life histories of the persons who achieved success.

Before conducting a study, one should know the realities related to life and those are:

- Struggles, difficulties, sorrows, sufferings, victories and defeats are all certain in one's life. All the above mentioned things will be always with you, with me and with everybody. In other words, these things were there, are there and will be there always.

  Accepting this fact, if we move ahead, then our lives will be comfortable. By accepting this fact, we will get ready psychologically to face injustice, defeats and frustrations that occur in our lives.

- It is in your hands what you want to become and how you want to shape your life!

Your psychological condition, physical condition and social status--everything depends upon the decisions you take and choices you make. Still if you want a better future, you have to make better choices and behave accordingly.

It is in your hands to have a better understanding regarding the aspects what you want to become, who you want to be like and what you want to achieve. Don't forget that the limitations which stand as obstacles and do not allow you to achieve what you want to achieve mostly come out of you.

In other words, you yourself are a hindrance for your own development, but not others.

'Necessity 'is the mother of invention, and 'Pain' is the father of learning.' So a person only after undergoing the difficult situations and frustrations will come to a conclusion that he should have a better life and try sincerely to achieve it.

Hence, in order to move forward in your life, you must always try to learn new things, get rid of the unnecessary things that are already with you and the things that you have learnt are causing harm.

Learn to Use Your Brain

The reason for many persons in the world who are drowned in frustrations without achieving success is never using their capabilities completely or not knowing how to use their capabilities...

For example: You got an expensive sophisticated computer as a gift from abroad. It was delivered at your home from your well-wishers. When you open the box and found everything except the instructional manual, and you don't have any computer training, then how can you operate the computer???

Even if you are an intelligent and wise person, it will take years to learn and operate the computer. Instead, when you have the instructional manual and the computer expert comes to your home and tells you how to operate it step by step, immediately you will be able to learn to operate the computer with complete efficiency. Isn't it??

So also, you come out of your mother's womb with a brain, like a computer. You don't know how to operate it (like without an instructional manual).

The brain is our primary control centre and a fantastically complex organ containing billions of neurons that can simultaneously process information from our bodies, operate our internal organs, generate thoughts and emotions, store and recall memories and control movements. When such a wonderful brain is properly used, it can make a pauper into a prince. It gives happiness, health, name and fame, etc.

This book is like an *instructional manual* that helps your brain to use it in a proper and systematic way like a *personal computer*. The book provides you with lots and lots of information, and this information will in turn help you to achieve what you want.

The persons who are confident like to take risks. By taking risks, they develop more confidence!

The Subconscious Mind – Thoughts

In your brain's computer, the subconscious mind is like a central processing unit. If you want to reach a goal, the thoughts, feelings and beliefs regarding the goal are reprogrammed into this unit andthen it will motivate you until you reach your goal.

So let's have a look how the Thoughts of the Subconscious Mind Works:

- When you have a thought, that thought leads you to have other thoughts. Finally, it will take you to the stream of consciousness and leads you away from your original thought.
- Then it will take you towards your goals that are deep in your heart or take you away from your goals. So everything depends upon your control over the mind.
- When you have thoughts, they introduce images regarding those thoughts into your mind.
- These thoughts and images wake up your emotions.
- These feelings sometimes wake up your thoughts and images and motivate them to get some more feelings or thoughts.
- Your thoughts, the images in your mind and your feelings motivate you to speak and work accordingly.

Two Types of Laws

There are two types of laws:

- Nature's laws
- Man-made laws

Nature's Laws: When we forgo the man- made laws, sometimes we may be caught or we may not be caught. But if we forgo the Nature's laws. We have to definitely face the repercussions.

Nature's laws are again sub-divided into two types:

- ❑ Physical laws
- ❑ Psychological laws

The equations regarding the physical laws are testified through experiments, like how to generate electricity, how to run the machines, etc.

But psychological laws are testified only through the experiences of life, applying the laws to life and through intuitions.

You should be positive and
optimistic towards life.
The more you are optimistic,
The more you gain confidence!

It is important for every person to know the psychological laws in order to achieve happiness and success in his life. When he applies these laws in his life, he can also exhibit self-discipline.

These laws are:

- ❑ To control yourself
- ❑ To search the reason for every result
- ❑ To be confident regarding your capabilities
- ❑ To expect that the work you are doing will yield you success
- ❑ To understand that the outer world is the image of your inner world

Let's look at them in detail:

To Control Yourself

The substance of this psychological law is that when you are able to control your life, then you feel positive!

If you don't have control on your life and some others control your life then you'll lose your self-confidence and feel negative.

So of all your primary responsibilities, the most important responsibility is to take control over your life. When you feel that you are having a total control over your life, it works as a foundation for your success and happiness.

To Search for the Reasons

Another law is that for every result we receive in our lives (it may be positive or negative result), there will be a reason!

When you achieve success or face failure, there are certain reasons. If you are healthy or sick, then also there are some reasons.

The popular proverb, "As you sow so shall you reap" is very much applicable here, because the actions or the thoughts of a person repay him the same kind.

Hence, first of all, you should confirm what you want to become or achieve in your life. Make your thinking accordingly in your mind and organise it systematically. Then you can ultimately achieve success.

Fear and distrust are the two big enemies that
don't allow us to achieve success!

To Be Self-Confident

The third thing is that when you are more confident, you can achieve more success. The confidence should be deep in your heart!

Positive & Negative Attitudes

Some people look at world with an 'optimistic attitude'. This type of people believe that the world is an ideal place to live. They see 'good' in everybody and in everything. They also believe that there are many opportunities around them to achieve success and believe that they are efficient even when they are not perfect. They have faith in everyone and believe in future with hope and confidence. They are basically called as **optimists** as they have a positive thinking.

Some people look at the with a 'pessimistic attitude'. This type of people believe that there is injustice, oppression and misfortune around them everywhere. They are unhappy with the people around them. This attitude keeps them away from self-esteem and self-love And they harbour negative feelings within them. Such persons are called pessimists and they do not achieve success easily remaining unhappy and unsatisfied throughout their lives with a pessimistic attitude!

Success is not the destiny,
but it is a journey!
There is more thrill in making
a positive journey to reach the destiny
than reaching the destiny!!

Expectations

Are you expecting some 'good' to happen today? How are you trying for that good to happen? If all the plans for 'today' go topsy-turvy and you face defeat.... Will you accept it decently and hopefully wait for 'tomorrow'? Have you learnt any lesson from today's failure?? When you expect with full confidence that the task you are doing will be completed, then definitely, it will completed.

Dr. Robert Rosenthal's Experiment

At the beginning of the school year, the principal called three teachers into his office and told that he has been observing the teaching methods of the teachers and identified that these three teachers were the best. As a gift, he wanted to give the responsibility of the special classes to these teachers. They then selected certain students for a particular class and the teachers were told that these students scored higher than average on the test and that was an indication that they were more likely to bloom during the school year.

At the end of the school year, all the students were tested. The results were very interesting. The students in the special class, the ones that had been labelled academic bloomers scored higher than the students at the same grade level in the other classes. The students were also rated higher on behavioural attributes. They were rated as more willing to learn, easier to get along with and in general, better students.

A Surprising Fact about the Experiment

The most interesting outcome from the experiment was the fact that the students in the special class were not selected based on the test scores. They were selected at random. The only real difference was the teachers' expectations from those students. This experiment was repeated over three hundred times and the results were all the same. The only difference between the special students and the other classes was the teachers believed that the students were capable of doing better and therefore, they did.

You tend to get from people what you expect of them. If you want people to perform better, to achieve more, then expect them to do so. Your expectations have a real bearing on the way people perform.

There are three types of expectations:

- **The Expectations of our Parents**

  We are all unconsciously programmed to the expectations of our parents. When they say, "my son becomes a great person" or "my son achieves" etc, all these remarks are absorbed into the subconscious mind and becomes as a belief and we try to be like that or live upto their expectations.. It also builds up the necessary self-confidence.

If parents nurture their children with negative expectations, the subconscious mind also responds negatively and the child grows up in an abnormal condition.

- **The Expectations of our Bosses**

  Your capabilities are testified according to the expectations of your Bosses. When your Boss speaks to you with positive expectations, you feel happy and work better. Even when you believe that your Boss has a good impression upon you, you tend to live upto his/her expectations and work hard.

  If your Boss speaks to you with negative expectations and discourages you, you will automatically work less than your capabilities. So the wise officers or bosses never talk ill of their subordinates.

- **The Expectations on Ourselves**

  This is our self-confidence. when we believe with full confidence that we can do the work we are assigned to, we do complete the work successfully.

  The expectation upon yourself is very powerful. It works as a talisman! With this expectation, you can bring out the best in you. You'll move forward positively, with an optimistic attitude and without hesitation, achieving success!

Organising Thoughts

You behave according to your thoughts, and according to your behaviour, you'll receive the results. So if you organise your thoughts, you can fulfil your wishes.

Your relationship with others depends according to your personality and the inner person in you. Your physical health depends according to your mental thinking. Your income, financial status, money, everything depends according to your plans and thoughts.

Many persons blame others for their misfortunes, sorrows and failures. They do not realise that their behaviour and thoughts are responsible for most of their mishaps and failures and never change their the ways of thinking and behaviour.

It is just like erasing the marks on the mirror when you actually have the marks on the image or the face. Instead one has to erase the marks on the face to actually get rid of the marks, once and for all.

Hence, when a person faces ups and downs, defeats and problems in his/her life, first of all, he/she has to change his/her thinking, attitude and behaviour..

This is the first step towards self-discipline. Then when you follow all the above-mentioned points step by step, you can finally achieve success.

Be Cool

(Peace of Mind)

To achieve Happiness and Success, one should be capable of managing the mental stress of one's day-to-day life.Your mind should be cool and peaceful to bring out the 'Best' from you. Peace of mind is an important aspect in one's life. All the success you achieve depends upon the peace of mind you have.

In order to achieve happiness in your personal or professional life, you should possess peace of mind.The opposite side of peace of mind is possessing negative emotions. Peace of mind makes your life happy and negative emotions make your life miserable. All the mental stress, tension and trauma that we face in our lives come out because of the negative emotions.

When you continue with these negative emotions, you fall sick physically or mentally, and may also lose your relationship with others.

Mental Stress

You can react to a situation in both ways, one that causes mental stress and the other that makes you simply forget the situation. So it's in your hands how to react to a particular incident or situation.

For example: Two persons were held up in a traffic jam on the same day, same time and same place. After some time, one person responded impatiently and angrily and the other person responded in a cool and relaxed manner.

The situation was the same, but the response of both the persons were different, one person was in mental stress and the other person was in no stress at all.

Generally, we all lose our mental peace because of not knowing the methods of stress management. Psychologists state that about 80% of physical sicknesses occur because of not knowing the methods of stress management.

High stress leads to dreadful and life threatening diseases like heart attacks, cancers, paralysis, ulcers, skin diseases, migraine, headaches, rheumatic pains, colitis and hyperthyroidism.

Good news is that mental stress is not a genetic disease! Through negative reaction to a particular situation, we feel a mental stress. The only remedy to relieve from mental stress is to be cool!

The most important aspect in stress management is to have control on yourself!

Seven Reasons

There are seven reasons that cause mental stress and negative emotions in a person. Around 95 to 99 percent unhappiness is because of the seven reasons mentioned below and they also tend to disturb the mental peace of a person. They are:

- ❑ Worrying
- ❑ No aim or goals in life
- ❑ Doing incomplete work
- ❑ Fear of failure
- ❑ Type 'A' behaviour
- ❑ Running away from a problem
- ❑ Anger

These seven aspects take away the mental peace of a person and cause mental stress. Now let us discuss them in detail.

Worrying

The primary aspect that causes mental stress is worrying! Feeling nervous about a thing, indecision, uncertainty, doubt, fear, tension, etc., are all characteristics of worry.

Worrying for everything is a disease and is hereditary, i.e., it comes from the parents to their children and so on. When a person always worries, his immunity system gets depressed and he or she is more prone to common ailments like cold, flu and other life threatening infections.

If a person wants to lead a happy life, first he should come out of worries, or stop worrying.

In a survey regarding the worries of a man, it revealed that the man usually worries due to the following reasons in the below mentioned percentages.

- About 40% worries are due to the things that don't happen
- 30% about the things in the past and for the things which can't be changed
- 12% about the sickness you have, or the sickness which can attack you anytime
- 10% about the unimportant things of life
- Out of 8%, 4% about the things that can never be done or not in one's control
- Only 4% worries that you have can actually solve your problems

Now examine your worries with the above said percentages and find out your worries are in which percentage.

Think of Today

Don't worry about yesterday or tomorrow, just think of today, or your present life.

If a person wants to be away from worries, he must live in the present and should not waste time by worrying about the past or the future. Just keep the following points always in your mind:

- Never postpone the things that are meant for today.
- Think of the things that can be done today.
- Complete the work that has to be done today itself.
- Be honest to yourself without any self-delusion.
- Everyday mould your life and feel it as an artistic piece. Always try to be creative in life.
- Help others.
- Read good books as books can be the best teachers and friends one can have.
- Always remember making friends is also an art.
- Foresee the hard days and be careful.....
- Never think of the things that will happen or never happen in the future.
- Then only one will be away from worries. There are four-fold programmes to come out of worries, if you follow them with a pure mind.

- First write about the problem that you are worrying on a paper clearly, sometimes while writing it you may find the solution for it.
- When you are unable to find the solution to a problem, think of the harm or loss done by it. This type of thinking helps you to reduce your stress.
- After having a clear-cut understanding regarding the loss or harm, you should be ready to accept it.
- Meanwhile, you have to put your efforts to reduce the loss. In business, it is called as 'Minimal Solution'!

John Paul Getty, one of the richest men in the world revealed some secrets to achieve success in the business like this-

"In every business matter, first you should assess the loss or damage and then take care to prevent that loss or damage….."

Write briefly about the problem that is disturbing you in a small notebook. Imagine that the problem is about your bosom friend and not yours. If your friend asks your advice for that problem, What are the solutions and advices that you suggest? Write the same solutions in front of your problem- So those are the solutions to your problem!! and then try to practise them.

Having Ideals

The second aspect that brings mental stress is meaningless life without any ideals. Life becomes arid when there is no aim or goal. About 80% of problems happen only because of your unawareness, you are unaware of what you want to achieve and not clear about your goals.

When you want to achieve 'something', in order to achieve that if you move forward with proper planning life will be thrilled. Even if you face problems in the middle of the way, you'll take them as a challenge but never feel stressed.

Likewise, if you don't have any aims and goals in your life, even minor problems gives you mental stress.

So in order to lead a meaningful and ideal life, sit aside, think and set at least ten goals for the coming twelve months. Write them on the paper, think how to achieve them and make a proper planning and move accordingly.

Writing about the goals, planning and decision making – all these aspects give you excitement, and this excitement improves your blood circulation and heart beat. You feel happy.

Doing Incomplete Work

The fourth stress causing aspect is unable to complete the task. Sometimes people feel difficult to complete their work and stop in the middle of it and are worried about their unfinished work. This leads to mental stress.

All of us want to finish the given task. When we complete the task, we are very much satisfied. Instead, if we fail to complete the task we feel dissatisfied and depressed.

Completing the work is like making a circle, incomplete work is like a semi circle.

Incomplete work makes us unhappy, always we think about the unfinished work and feel mental stress, this leads to depression, anger, sleeplessness etc.

The solution for this problem is completing the unfinished work immediately without any pending. To do this one needs self-discipline.

By inculcating self-discipline in your life, you can complete all the pending tasks. This gives you happiness and self-satisfaction. Further your self-esteem increases and you feel positive.

Fear of Failures

One of the aspects that make us feel mental stress is fear of failure. Hesitation, fear, unable to make decisions, worrying etc are all the different forms of fear.

When you have a fear in your mind that "I can't do this", then you feel insecure. This will affect your digestive system.

Fear of failure suppresses the capabilities of an individual, in other words all the talents and capabilities of an individual are wasted.

It is natural to an individual to have some fear at certain point of time. The definition for courage is amusing it goes like this:

The person who moves forward without any fear is not courageous. However, the person who moves forward even with the fear in his mind is courageous.

There is a simple solution for the people who want to achieve success in their life:

"First decide what you want to achieve and what you want to become, and move forward thinking that failure is impossible in achieving it!"

You have to behave that you don't have any fear. At least, you have to pretend like that.

Ask yourself by questioning, "If there is no fear how do I behave in this situation?". Behave accordingly and move forward courageously.

Remember one thing

"Failure is not an end. Failure teaches a lesson, which is useful to achieve success!"

Many great persons in the history conquered the fear of failure and achieved success in their life.

The quality of victorious is to move forward confidently, by pushing back the fear of failure.

"Failures are the stepping stones for success!"

Life should be like a 'treasure'

But it shouldn't be like a 'treasure hunt'!

Type 'A' Behaviour

The fifth aspect that causes mental stress is - Type 'A' Behaviour.

Type 'A' persons are always emotional, they react for trivial matters and feel stress, they are aggressive, they don't have control over themselves, they can't enjoy life and always in a hurry.

Because of their aggressive nature, they are prone to hypertension, even in the situations where they have to behave in a normal way they become aggressive. There is a heavy blood pressure in this type 'A' persons.

This heavy blood pressure burdens the hearts that pumps the blood and in long run, the heart becomes weak. Then this type of 'A'- persons are prone to heart diseases and paralysis.

Type 'A' persons always boast about their achievements, valuables, savings and income. They always compare with others. Especially with their colleagues (if they are employees), with other businesspersons. They want to be ahead than others.

Type 'A' persons have low self-esteem. They have insecurity feeling – says Mayor Freedman, a cardiologist from San Francisco.

Type 'A' persons are hard working people. This is the reason why American companies prefer to take these persons. With their hard work they become 'Burn-Out'. Again, they will try to take fresh type 'A' persons into their companies.

Type 'A' Behaviour is not at all an acceptable quality. Because of this behaviour, man looses mental peace. Therefore, people with this type have to try to change their behaviour. Some of the solutions are:

First, accept that you have type 'A' behaviour. Understand that because of this behaviour you are losing mental peace and happiness.

Take a strong decision regarding that behaviour you have to change.

Some people feel proud of their Type 'A' Behaviour, but it's not correct. Because of this behaviour they are losing their life span 15-20 years. It's a foolish thing, not changing the behaviour which reduces the life span.

Get relaxed. Make it a habit, allot 20 minutes daily both morning and evening. Relaxation may be through meditation or exercise. Even through sitting lonely and listening music.

Still if you need further information regarding type 'A' behaviour you can get it from the book "**Stress Management**" (written by the author).

Life is the image of your thoughts.
If you change your thoughts, your
life will also change.

Type 'A' Personality & Workaholics

There are another set of people, who behave equally like **Type 'A' persons**. They are called as workaholics. This second set of people also work hard like type 'A' people but there is a lot of difference between these two types.

Type 'A' persons never feel that they have control over the work they do. They work to satisfy others or they work for others when they are asked.

But workaholics are not like this, they never work for others or to satisfy others. They work only to reach their goals, which they are bound. Through that work, they feel exceptional satisfaction.

Workaholics can work even 10, 12, 14 hours daily. Even with this same spirit they can work whole week. Unlike type 'A' persons this type of persons after reaching their goal, will enjoy their vacation without any work. They never think of other work during those days. They never worry about anything.

Workaholics make use of all their talents and capabilities and work for the things that are vital to them. They are positive, they will not have anger, vengeance and repentance. They are always happy and delighted. Generally they take up the tasks, which they like and which gives pleasure.

Type 'A' persons are not like this. They never take pleasure in the work. They work with tension and they have negative thinking.

Now think which type you belong or you may be the person who doesn't like to do any work......

Running Away from Problems

The sixth aspect, which takes away mental peace and causes mental stress is –running away from the problem.

Regarding, success there are two types of persons:

- The people who face the problem
- The people who run away from the problem

A famous university made an experiment with the persons who have the above said two types of mentalities.

- Under first group they have taken the people who run away from the problems and kept them in a room. Electrodes were fixed on everybody's bodies, for every 60 seconds they were given minor current shocks through the electrodes.

  A wall clock was hung on the wall so that every student can see it. So whenever the clock hand which shows seconds, reaches 12 they were given current shock.

  A video camera was fixed in that room so that the facial feelings of the students can be seen.

  So whenever this group saw clock hand reaching 12, they use to turn their face with pain.

  After the experiment it was recorded that their heartbeat, B.P and respiration increased to 30 to 40%

  This group has undergone mental stress during the current shock.

- Later they have taken the second group who face the problems and experimented same experiment.

  The second group whenever they saw the clock hand reaching 12, they saw it boldly without turning their face with fear. When their heartbeat, B.P and respiration was examined it recorded normal.

  By this we can understand that the people who run away from the problem, when they face a problem, undergo mental stress. But the people who face the problem, when they face a problem take it as a challenge and never feel stressed.

So, when you face a problem honestly, without any fear – move forward systematically and then only you'll be confident. You'll be shrewd in overcoming all situations and facing all kinds of competitions.

So in your job or in personal life, whenever you face unpleasant situations, never feel sad, or depressed.

You have to mould your desires according to your life and never feel sad that your life is not up to your desires.

Your sole aim should be to possess mental peace in your life, so accordingly mould your life around the mental peace that you shave created or achieved.

Anger

The seventh aspect, which destroys mental peace and arouses negative feelings in the people is anger!

Of all the negative emotions, the most damaging emotion is anger. This anger results in heart attacks, paralysis, ulcers, migraine, headaches, different types of skin diseases and blast of blood vessels.

Uncontrolled anger destroys the marital relations, relations between the kith and kin, individuality of the growing children and employment of a person.

All your luck depends upon your efforts.

So the more efforts you make

makes you the most luckiest!

The most remarkable aspect about the anger is that it is not at all a useful emotion to the man, because it never does 'good' to anybody.

The most destructive negative emotion is anger!

If you want you can be away from it, because anger comes out from the mind. So if you know how to be cool you can't get anger.

The emotion you choose to a particular situation as a response is anger!

In difficult situations, you can be cool and positive or you can revolt with anger. You are free to choose one out of these two options. So think carefully......

Create the situations for yourself, but

never become slaves to the situations.

This is what self-control means!!

Aspects That Make You Angry

Some type of grievance upon a person or a thing causes anger. Sometimes we get anger when the things don't happen or the people act according to our will. Anger enacts the fight or flight response in our brain, which increases our blood pressure and releases adrenaline into our bloodstream, thereby increasing our strength and pain threshold. Anger makes us think of only two things: Defend, Attack.

However, if anger is left uncontrolled and free to take over the mind and body at any time, then anger becomes destructive.

Take two decisions.The First thing to control the anger in you.

The Second thing is to stop being angry as a response to the things you don't like.!!

Be obstinate as much as possible and don't come to a conclusion without a thorough evaluation of a person or a thing. Never try to put the blame on others. Instead, think peacefully about your role in it.

Only peaceful and constructive thinking keeps you away from anger.

Reduce the Anger through Touch

If you are angry, you can reduce it through touch. By touching an object with your legs, hands and teeth firmly, you can reduce your anger. In other words, by hitting or kicking an object firmly, you can reduce your anger. But do not throw things to display your anger. The best games to reduce your anger and mental stress are: Handball, Volleyball, Basketball, Football, Badminton, Tennis, etc.

Most of the teenagers face the problem of pimples because of the suppressed anger in them. They can overcome this problem through playing the above mentioned games and releasing their suppressed anger.

Another amazing aspect is that games like running, swimming and cycling never help to reduce the anger, but they generally help to reduce weight and mental stress, because in these games there is no chance of touch.

Chewing is also another important way to reduce your anger, because you can feel the touch of the object in between your teeth. Cricket is the best example. In cricket, we usually observe the players chewing bubble gums vigorously to release their frustrations, anger and tensions.

Shouting will also helps to release the anger, but it is not recommended at all. Sometimes we observe people fighting or kicking one another, hitting and shouting at one another, if not biting one another. All these are symptoms of extreme anger.

Therefore, when you release your anger by exhibiting it upon other things, you'll be free from anger and have peace of mind but you have to be careful about the way you let out your anger or frustration. If you overcome the seven aspects mentioned above, then you will lead a stress-free life and have peace of mind. By being cool and having peace of mind, you can utilise your capabilities completely and ultimately achieve success.

So, Be cool - Be positive- and Move Forward to reach your goal! Definitely, you can achieve success.....

Bad Habits-Good Habits

The habits, which are bad will take you away without helping you to achieve success and the habits, which are good will take you towards achieving success. So after you are able to differentiate between the good and the bad habits, try to keep away from the bad habits by inculcating the good habits in your life and you can achieve success.

Bad Habits

- To feel that you are poor and miserable
- Fear of sickness
- Laziness
- Envy
- Greediness
- Boasting
- Criticising everything
- Living life without a goal or aim and just believing in destiny
- Impatience
- Vengeance
- Jealousy
- Lack of honesty
- Craziness
- Sadistic nature

Good Habits

- Living with a goal and aim: It is the primary requisite in your life. This quality makes you alert and increases your will power.
- Confidence: Your mind should be always filled with positive feelings and away from negative feelings and fears. This will help you to form self-discipline.
- Daring nature: You should be brave enough to take trisks or dare to move ahead to achieve your goal/goals without waiting for others to tell you to proceed.

- ❑ Happiness: It is something in within – a feeling that can be felt only when you move forward to achieve your goals with a new spirit and inspiration.
- ❑ Self-discipline: The more you practise self-discipline, the more opportunities it will bring for your achieving success in your life. So march ahead and all the best!

Optimism

If there is half litre water in a one litre tumbler, person 'A' says like this....

"Half of the tumbler is filled with water."

Person 'B' says about the same thing as....

"Half of the tumbler is empty."

In this regard, 'A' is an optimist and 'B' is a pessimist.

Two sailors are sailing away from their way and they see a shore at a distance. The first sailor says "I am afraid of the cannibals on that shore," and the second sailor says that "Cheer up friend! It could be a heaven!" The first sailor is a pessimist, whereas, the second sailor is an optimist.

Basically, an optimist searches for an opportunity even in danger, whereas, a pessimist searches for danger even in his opportunities. Life will be colourful for the optimists and life seems dull and boring for the pessimists.Although, both of them have their own abilities.

However, sometimes optimists can go wrong and pessimists can be practical.

Optimists look at life with an optimistic attitude. They recognise the charm of life and wait for the radiance with hope, whereas, Pessimists view every aspect with a negative approach and feel depressed. They look at the darker side of life.

Almost in everybody, we find both the optimistic and the pessimistic feelings. Some people in the world are with extra optimism and some are with extra pessimism.

Pessimists feel that they were responsible for the failures and blame themselves. Optimists never agree and feel that they were responsible for their failures and even if they held themselves responsible, they are positive and believe in the proverb that 'failures are the pillars of success'..

The only advantage for the pessimists is that they do not expect anything from the world, so they never feel sad. With this attitude, they lose many opportunities and sometimes, they lose the profits that they are supposed to get.

Whenever, pessimists face failure, grief increases in them and life seems very boring. They develop fear, anger, depression, sadness and sorrow towards their life, whereas, optimists are people, who even when they face failures, move forward with a hope that someday they will achieve success. They take up new programmes and develop new and innovative ideas with that hope. Even with all the difficulties and frustrations, life seems fresh to the optimists and dull to the pessimists.

Hope – Optimism

There is no big difference between desire and optimism. '**Hope**' bestows the essential capabilities to fulfil their dreams. '**Optimism**' gives the essential motivation to a person to move forward without any sadness even when a sad situation takes place!

The advantages are the same with both '**Hope**' and '**Optimism**'.

Optimism – Pessimism

When you are on your way to the office and come across your boss, you wish him, 'Good Morning'. Without any response, he goes away. This makes you think that your Boss is angry or upset with you and may shout at you with some reason or the other after you enter the office. Well, if you think like this, then you are a pessimist. When you listen to a lecture of a politician and think, "All the politicians are frauds and foolish people" then too, you are a pessimist!

The main quality of the pessimists is that they think that all the failures and bad situations in life are permanent and it's impossible to change them. However, optimists are never like this. They feel that all the failures and bad situations in life are temporary and it's always possible to change them.

Let's read an example related to these types of persons:

Vivek and Sudha – both husband and wife are working in a private company. Because of some reasons, the company removed them from their jobs. Later their reactions are like this...:

Vivek felt very bad. He stopped caring about his wife and child, left home and began wandering with friends. Even he stopped jogging which was his daily activity. He caught hold of cold and suffered from it throughout that season.

Sudha was not like this. She remained the same. She did her daily activity of skipping. Her health was not affected. She spent her days without any sickness.

So here, we can say that Vivek is a Pessimist. He felt sad and frustrated when he lost his job. It affected his life and health whereas, Sudha was not like this. She was an optimist. She felt sad for losing her job, but she had overcome her sadness with an optimistic attitude.

Later again, the company asked them to join in their jobs. Then Sudha thought - "They must have recognised my value, so they didn't want to lose me."

But, Vivek thought "They were unable to find another employee, that's why they were calling me again!"

So......

Optimists think that failures and bad situations never last long. They are temporary for some particular situations and then they change.

But pessimists think that all the failures and bad situations are permanent and it's impossible to change them. Pessimism makes a person depressed.

Optimism – Health

The people with optimism live longer than the people with pessimism.

A Psychologist, Christopher Peterson at the University of Michigan studied the behaviour of 172 students for a year and observed that pessimists are often prone to Flu and Throat infections than the optimists. The study also revealed that....

- Pessimists consulted doctors more number of times than the optimists.
- Optimists are young and energetic even in their middle age. They live long. But pessimists suffer from heart attacks, cancers and hypertensions and live a short span of life.

A study on 100 heart patients from San Francisco hospital revealed that the patients with optimistic attitude have less chances of getting heart attacks for the second time.

For example, out of 16 optimistic patients who got heart attacks for the first time, 11 are surviving even after 8 years, whereas, out of 16 pessimistic heart patients, only 1 person is surviving after 8 years.

For pessimists, there are more chances of undergoing depressions. Depression weakens the immune system. So pessimists are more prone to different types of diseases.

A Ph.D psychologist C.R Snyder from Kansas University, after a thorough evaluation says like this:

"If you have small hope in your mind, it fills tons of energy into your body."

Yes, it's true!

The Principles to Become Optimistic

The above mentioned aspects reveal that it is good for every person to live with an optimistic attitude!

But here is a doubt-

Can a person with pessimistic approach, be changed into optimistic approach??

Yes, he can!

But it can't be happen within a day or night.....

Following are some principles to be optimistic:

- ❑ In every pessimist, there will be a negative critic. He will discourage and make you mentally weak for every minute failure and misfortune. So first of all, shut the mouth of that negative critic. The chapter, "Away from Negative Thoughts" from this same book will be helpful to you in this aspect.
- ❑ Think how will you imagine the word ,'Hope'?

  Just like a simple word without any substance ?

  Or

  As a meaningful word which fills new happiness in your life??

  How do you define the glass with half-filled water?

  'Glass with half-filled water' or 'Glass with half of the water emptied'??

If you feel that it is a 'Glass with half of the water emptied' then you are having negative thoughts. But if you feel that it is a glass with half of the water emptied, then you are a pessimist. Basically, it is always advisable to look at the better side or the positive side of life. By doing so, you will gain and get better results.

- ❑ When you are sad and dull, do the exercises that give you physical strength. Exercises make you energetic and active.

- A sound body has a sound mind, and Happiness, Health and Sound Mind are interlinked with one another.
- When you are sad and discouraging, take up some constructive activity.
- Draw a picture or do gardening work or watch a comedy movie or prepare your favourite dish. Involve in some activity which gives you happiness.....
- Always be constructive with positive and innovative thoughts, new plans, etc. Try to implement those new plans, taking up a new job/assignment, or meeting some unfamiliar persons. Whatever they may be.....
- Those plans should give you happiness and success, because the success achieved from the tiny goals encourage you to win a big victory.
- Never have doubts in your mind thinking that is it possible to generate good results only through optimism? Because:
    - Your optimism of today in the forthcoming days will be an 'investment' for your life.

Pandora's Box

There is a beautiful story in Greek mythology regarding optimism in man. According to it:In Greek mythology, there was a woman called Pandora. She was given a beautiful container by the gods, which she was not to open under any circumstance. Impelled by her curiosity, Pandora opened it and all evil contained therein escaped and spread over the earth. She hastened to close the container, but the whole contents had escaped, except one thing that lay at the bottom was '**Hope**'!

Today, only this hope is leading the man towards achieving success!!

This story regarding 'Hope' is apt with the results of the scientific experiments done by the present day's psychologists. Therefore,

> *"A wise man watches his faults closely than his virtues; fools reverse the order."*
>
> – Napoleon Hill

Get Ready for the Success

According to a survey, an ordinary man in his complete lifespan is utilising only 10% of his capabilities. Even one of the famous intellectuals of the 20th century, Sir Albert Einstein has also utilised only 15% of his mental capabilities, a research study confirmed examining his brain after death.

This means you or me or we – all are wasting 90-98 percent of our capabilities.

This is a surprising aspect!!

So also-

In the history from the first man to modern man, nobody resembles alike. It's impossible to look alike.

So you are a very special person, isn't it?!

As a special person, you can also do some special things that are impossible to others.

But are you doing those things??

It's a fact that only very few people in the world are born with extraordinary talents. We have to accept that many of us start our life with normal wisdom, talents and capabilities.

Majority of the people – both male and female achieved success in the special field they chose, only by improving their normal talents with hard work. They can't achieve such sort of success if they sat in a corner lazily without putting any efforts.

So identify your capabilities and talents, analyse them, and then try to achieve success through improving them.

Potentialities of a Person

There is an equation regarding the potentialities of person:

(Your own talents+ the skills which are acquired through learning) x your attitude = potentialities performed by you.

It's simply:

(A+B) x C= D

'A' is your talent acquired by you genetically from your ancestors and parents. This you can't change.

'B' is your skill acquired through your education and experiences.

'C' is your attitude towards life. If you have normal own talents (A) and normal acquired skills (B), when you improve the quality of your attitude then you can achieve wonderful results.

It is also known as Positive Mental Attitude.

Attitude

You can improve your attitude whenever you want and as much as you want. How much success you achieve in your life depends upon your positive attitude than your mind.

Don't forget that the attitude is under the direct control of your mind or will. Attitude is nothing but your way of approach towards the life.

'Positive Attitude' means the way you feel that all things work together for good and feeling happy with that hope!

Facing the day-to-day situations cheerfully is **'Positive Attitude'**!

Your 'attitude' is the mirror of your 'character'. The people around you will respond according to your attitude.

Attitude is shaped according to your expectations. These expectations are formed according to your 'beliefs'.

Your beliefs will control the quality of your personality.

These beliefs are shaped according to your self-concept.

Self-Concept

Self-Concept is in your subconscious mind just like a 'Master Programme' in the computer.

Your self-concept regulates your life.

The awareness you have on various aspects that are related to you and your life is known as overall self-concept.

Three Types of Self-Concept

For any person, there are **three types of self-concept**:

First: Self-Ideal

Second: Self-Image

Third: Self-Esteem

When these three aspects are combined in a person, it becomes his **self-concept**.

Let's discuss about each aspect:

The First Aspect of Self-Concept is Self-Ideal

Self-ideal is nothing but what you want to be and how you would like to be.

Unfortunately, many persons do not have self-ideal. Even the persons who have self-concept don't have clear opinion and live a wavering life. Due to the lack of self-improvement, they can't achieve anything in their life.

Any person in order to possess self-improvement and self-development he should certainly need self-ideal. He should have a natural desire towards the ideals, which he wants to manifest them through his character. This is one of the basic factors to achieve success!

The Second Aspect of Self-Concept is Self-Image

You can feel your self-image as an **'Inner Mirror'**.

Your qualities, your opinions and the way you react to situation etc... All these aspects are reflected in your 'Inner Mirror' or Self-Image.

Your opinion about what you want to be and how you want to behave will be according to your self-image.

You can change your self-image by changing your walk, talk and the way you react. Even you can change your behaviour.

By doing so, you can also improve your performance and achieve success.

The Third Aspect of Self-Concept is Self-Esteem

The way what you feel about your self is your self-esteem. This is an emotional aspect of your personality. (Already we have dealt about this in the previous chapters

Based on two things you can understand how much self-esteem you have upon yourself..

- **First aspect which decides your self-esteem** – It is your personal assessment. By thinking how valuable you are, by feeling how skilled & rightful you are and how much you are accepting yourself as a good person. Even when you face many trials and tribulations in this world, you'll not let down the opinion upon yourself as a human being. You are a person with high moral values.

- **Second aspect which decides your self-esteem** - Your belief upon your potentialities!

  Your self-confidence also depends upon this aspect.

  There is a close relationship between these two aspects that are related to the self-esteem.

  When you have high opinion upon yourself, you can display better performance. When you display better performance, you can form a high opinion upon yourself. So both the aspects are very important.

  In order to know your self-esteem you have to self-examine yourself.

The more you'll become confident the more you like yourself. You'll move forward with a positive attitude. You'll also improve your health, potentialities and happiness.

When you can't love yourself you can't love others. Others also can't love you.

These are the basic aspects of self-esteem!

Programme your Thoughts towards Success

Your present position and the present status depend upon the plans made by you in the past. By controlling your conscious mind and your thoughts, you can shape your future as you like it. The strong desire to have better future disciplines your mind. You'll also make your thoughts accordingly to achieve it.

But all this can't happen in one day, without displeasure you have to try until you succeed.

In order to change your present condition you have to change your thoughts and your life style.

Is it easier to change our habitual actions??

To understand it we have to know certain basics about the habits.

Habits and its Functions

In Physics, Newton's first law of motion is:

"A body at rest tends to remain at rest, and a body in motion tends to remain in motion, unless acted upon by an outside force"

So also, all your habitual actions and thoughts work according to this theory. Unless some outside force controls you, you'll behave in the same old manner. To change your behaviour and thoughts you have to take some strict decisions.

When you struck up in your habitual actions and behaviour, in your life you'll will be-

- ❑ Stuck up in the same job
- ❑ Continue same business and meet same people
- ❑ Eat the same variety of food
- ❑ Go to the office in the same route
- ❑ View the same daily programmes in the T.V
- ❑ Read same type of books
- ❑ All the daily activities happen in a routine way –no change in any of these things.

It is good until these habits enrich your happiness and victories in your life. But when they stand as an obstacles in your happiness and success, definitely you have to change your habits. You have to modify your habits.

According to Shakespeare- "There is no good or no evil in the world only it's in our thinking"

So if you can change thoughts you can change your life.

Your way of responding to situation decides your success or failure, happiness or sorrow.

Remember –

- ❑ It's easier to acquire bad habits but it's difficult to live with those bad habits
- ❑ It's difficult to acquire good habits but it's easier to live with those good habits.

Change your Habits through Practice

Habits are acquired through learning so we can change them through patience and practice.

First, we should have a strong 'desire' to change those habits.

In order to acquire a new habit, practice it as practice makes perfect.

According to your constructive thinking and actions, the people around you and the situations will change. This offers you a remarkable success.

The Influence of Emotions

Emotions strengthen our thoughts or the emotional thoughts are very powerful.

Emotion is like electricity, fire. You can use it for constructive purpose or destructive purpose.

It's not correct as some of them imagine that we are 90% emotional & 10% rational. We are cent per cent emotional.

It is natural that every task we do is influenced by sort of emotion.

There are two types of emotions:

- ❑ Desire
- ❑ Fear

All the things that we do or don't depend upon these two emotions.

It's a fact to remember that there are many things which are undone with the 'fear' than the things which are done with the 'desire'.

Thoughtless emotions give frustration to a person.

Three Aspects that Require to be Changed

- ❑ You should have a sincere 'desire' to change. The 'desire' to be in a better condition than what you are in, should always ignite your mind until you achieve it.
- ❑ The second aspect is 'wish'.
  Many of them want to change their life but in their heart, they won't 'wish' for it. They are happy with their previous life and previous friends.
  You should 'wish' to become or be ready to become a 'new person' by shifting the 'old person' in you.
- ❑ The third aspect is 'trying to do the things' that are important towards making a change.
  It takes a long time to get the result. Sometimes it may take years. You have to work hard. You should be ready to accept this....

"BE WHAT YOU WANT TO BE."

"Victory comes only to those who work long and hard,
Who are willing to pay the price in blood, sweat and tears".

— Winston Churchill

SECTION - II
CONDUCT MANAGEMENT

First Impression is the Best Impression

You meet a stranger. He doesn't know anything about you. You talk to him. He forms an opinion about you. Do you know how much time does he take to form an opinion?

Firts Four Minutes

Only in four minutes, he will frame an opinion about you. What sort of person are you? What type of personality do you have? Is it good to make friendship with you are not? Whether you are an optimist or pessimist? etc.. He will imprint these thoughts about you in his mind.

Whenever he meets you, these thoughts will work as a Bias. These thoughts will guide him whenever he responds to you.

For example, in the first impression itself, if he believes that you are not a reliable person, all the efforts to become close to him doesn't change his mind. He will always maintain a distance with you.

If he believes that you are a kind- hearted and friendly person, nobody can change his mind, even if some people talk badly about you.

Opinions become Beliefs

A person, when he forms an opinion in the first four minutes, turns it as a belief and this lasts long in his mind throughout his life.

It may be a good opinion or bad, but once if it turns as a belief, nobody can erase it. So we should always strive to give the best impression in the first sight itself.

Now, let's look at some examples regarding these beliefs:

Generally, we see different types of people like fat persons, slim persons and the persons with different attitudes. The beliefs that have rooted strongly in the society from the primitive days upon these type of people are:

- If we look at a fat person, we think that he is jovial and easy go lucky person.
- If we look at a lean person, we think that he is nervous, may be deceptive and we should be careful with him.
- If we look at person with spectacles, we think that he may be good at studies and intelligent.
- If we look at a tall person, we feel that he is energetic and romantic.
- Short persons may be cunning.
- When we a look at a woman with lot of outward show and pomp, we feel that she has a lose character, a woman without brains and her outward beauty is a meagre waste.

In reality, these are all wrong beliefs. They are Bias- these above said beliefs will not be applicable to all. Even we know about it, still when we look at these kinds of people, immediately, we remember these biased thoughts.

Basically, First Impressions have a Strong Impact.

The first impression that we form in the first four minutes on a person is very strong, so instead of forming a negative impression, isn't it better to form a positive impression?.

For that, we should always be careful with our dressing, talking and with our behaviour. Even if we have any defects, we can set them right. By doing so, we can do good to ourselves.

To form the first impression on a person, what aspects of that person play a prominent role and to what extent?

The Way We Glance (scan) at a Person

When we meet a person, we glance at his face, especially his eyes and mouth. (Look at the Picture of a Person).

While talking to person (he may be a familiar person or stranger), we glance at his body in the following manner.

- 75% at his eyes and mouth
- 10% at his forehead and hair

- ❑ 5% at his chin
- ❑ 10% at the remaining part of his body

Even while talking to a person, whom we meet for the first time, we scan him in the same manner. Especially, we glance specifically in the first three seconds.

So in order to create a good impression upon others, we should:

- ❑ 90 % be careful with our facial expressions and the way we speak
- ❑ 10% be careful with our dressing, walking and our behaviour

What all the expressions that we express unknowingly, are automatically acquired from our surroundings, where we spent our childhood. But we can change those expressions positively with patience and self-discipline.

So also even our walking and behaviour are also according to our surroundings, where we are nurtured. We can change them through discipline.

Whatever we may be, by birth or through our nurturing, if we have a strong desire to lead a successful life among others and achieve victory- we can win anyone only through our efforts, discipline and through the available modern equipments.

By doing so, even we can mould the society accordingly and get the positive results.

To achieve this, what you have to do is discussed in the further pages....

"I am the Master of my fate,
I am the Captain of my soul."

— W.E. Henly

How to Earn Money

Now, you have a strong desire to earn and earn a lot!

This is not only your wish. Everyone in the world has the same wish.

But only wishing is not enough, you have to put your efforts to fulfil your wish.

When you are planning to earn a lot of or a considerable amount of money:

- ❑ First have a clear-cut idea regarding the figure you want to earn.
- ❑ Make a proper planning to earn that money. Write it on a paper and also write the reason, why you want to earn that money.
- ❑ Write down from which date you want to start your efforts and on which date you want to finish that task.

- ❑ Sign on the paper, where you made this planning and write down the date. This is a contract, which you made to yourself.
- ❑ Read you plan again and underline the things that are standing as obstacles in front of you and not allowing you to move forward according to your planning. Write those underlined things into second list.
- ❑ Complete every task one by one, written in the second list. Some tasks may be repeated daily.
- ❑ Daily read that paper which contains your planning. You have to be well-versed with it. Whatever work you do, always remember your planning.
- ❑ Your goal of planning should be like this…

"Hereafter within six months, I '….' have to earn this much money. For that I will have to do so and so and X Y Z tasks… etc.."

Improve Your Image

(Positive Image)

To achieve success in life, first we have to create a good impression in others about us. We have to project a good image in others' minds. This good image is also called as **positive image**.

A positive image not only projects your external appearance like make up and dressing, but also projects your physical and mental health.

Regular exercises, nutritious food, peace of mind and disciplined life, etc will help you to improve your image.

Health

There is a close relationship between health and beauty. If a person is not healthy, he doesn't look good even if he/she is handsome or beautiful.

But when the person is healthy, he looks good even he/she is not handsome or beautiful. In order to have good health, one should take nutritious food that contains vitamins and minerals. Deficiency of vitamins and minerals will take away your charm. For example, if a person:

- Suffers with the deficiency of vitamin B-1 (Thiamine), he can't bear the slightest sound.
- Deficiency of Riboflavin results in depression.
- Lack of calcium results in fatigue.

So one has to take healthy food and a balanced diet which contains proteins and carbohydrates. Fresh leafy vegetables and fruits will also enrich the health of a person.

Exercises

Regular exercises not only make you fit, but also help you to maintain a good physique. Running is the best exercise!

To make running a habit, first four days walk half an hour. Later three weeks, walk for some time and run for some time. Slowly, reduce the walk and increase the run. It looks like a simple exercise, but it creates wonders in our life.

Sleep

Exercises helps us to burn the calories in our body. Sleep refreshes our mind and body. Daily make it a habit of going to bed at an exact time, so that the body will also adjust accordingly. Hot water shower or a glass of hot milk or reading a good book will help us to get sound sleep. Timely sleep and timelygetting up early in the morning makes our body and mind healthy and fresh, and it also makes our face glow.

Quietness

When you sit aside ten to twenty minutes, twice a day keeping your mind blank and relax your body, it will make your face spark and glow. You will also have a good health.

Stop drinking tea, coffee and smoking, instead roam here and there. Make it a habit of listening melodious music.

Observing silence is also a great experience. By inculcating quietness in life, we feel happy and confident.

Grooming

To look beautiful only by dressing is not sufficient. You should also groom yourself. Grooming means not only shaving or taking shower or sparkling the teeth, you should also take care of different parts of your body. For example:

Feet

We should take care of our feet. Many times, we are careless of our feet. Regularly, we have to do pedicure. Keeping the feet in hot water with some shaving lotion in it for 10 minutes will help our feet to become clean and refreshed.

We should also be careful about our footwear before buying them. Cut the toenails regularly with a good nail cutter and have a straight cut.

Hands

The person who wants to look beautiful should also take care of his hands. Regularly, manicure them and apply body lotion. Once in a week cut your fingernails.

Teeth

The food you take and your age has a great impact on your teeth. Daily, you have to brush your teet and once in six months, you muat consult the dentist. Take food that is rich in fibre, and which contains vitamin 'C', 'B' complex and calcium and the tip of your brush should be small with soft bristles.

Skin

The skin of our body is seen first by others. It undergoes many changes according to the seasons. Growing age, Temperature, Pollution and Smoking have negative effect on our skin.

To have a soft skin it is important to drink about eight glasses of water, and take bath regularly. This will keep the skin clean.

Hair

Hair is considered to be one of the beautiful assets that a person possesses. Healthy hair is a sign of beauty, vitality and youth. Eat well, exercise regularly and get enough sleep to reduce stress levels. Stress can cause hair loss. Eat a balanced amount of protein every day and be sure to take adequate amounts of iron and zinc!

Reasons for Most of Our Failures

The following are the reasons that lead a man towards failures. If any habit is applicable to you, try to change those habits:

- ❑ To lead a carefree life without having a goal and destination
- ❑ To show unnecessary worry towards others' issues
- ❑ Lack proper education
- ❑ Unable to control the desires, looking down upon the opportunities- resulting in lack of self-discipline
- ❑ Lack of goals and ideals
- ❑ Negative thoughts resulting in ill-health
- ❑ Childhood bad habits and bad influences
- ❑ Lack of boldness

- ❑ Negative attitude
- ❑ Unable to control the anger
- ❑ Wishing something to happen without efforts
- ❑ Unable to take the timely decisions
- ❑ Fear of death, criticism, ill-health, losing love, old age, losing freedom, death, etc....
- ❑ Poor selection in choosing the partner
- ❑ Too cautious or too careless
- ❑ Unable to use the vacation
- ❑ Wasting time and money
- ❑ Unable to control the tongue
- ❑ Impatience
- ❑ Unable to live with others
- ❑ Unable to sustain confidence
- ❑ Lack of foreseeing (Imagination)
- ❑ Boasting and self-appraisal
- ❑ Vengeance
- ❑ Laziness and fatigue

Achievers of Success- Their Style

Success Formula-1

The style of the persons who achieve success is different. They lead their life in a special way. Examine the following qualities and assess whether you possess any one of these qualities:

- ❑ Positive attitude
- ❑ Self-confidence
- ❑ Concentration
- ❑ Having a goal and an ambition
- ❑ Ability to face failures
- ❑ Commitment

Let's examine them in detail:

- ❑ The persons who achieve success will not have 'fear of failure'. They will be of positive expectation. They are always in a positive attitude.
- ❑ "I can do this" is the feeling of a person who possesses self-confidence. Without out self-confidence no one can achieve anything.

- To achieve your goal you need lot of concentration.
- Life becomes wayward without any goal or ambition. It means to know what you want. First, you have to set short-term goals and achieve success by doing so you can achieve your long-term goals.
- Successful persons always accept failures as feedback. Failure seems them as delayed success but not as failure. One has to analyse the reasons for the failures and take care not to repeat it again.
- Commitment is also called as determination. Without caring the obstacles or hardships and moving forward to reach the goal is the chief characteristic of a successful person.

Do you possess these qualities???

Self-discipline – lesson-2

Whenever we talk of self-discipline, immediately, we recall of Mahatma Gandhi. He is one of the greatest personalities of this century. He hasn't owned any house or money. This poor man frightened the Great British Empire. Where did he get that power??

Following are the five aspects that made him a powerful person:.

- Having an aim in life: Mohandas Karamchand Gandhi had an aim to bring independence to India. He had a definite purpose.
  - He knew his aim and he was so determined that no power in the world could defeat him.
- Selfless Life: Gandhiji always lead a very special life. No one paid him for leading that kind of life. He himself chose 'that' life.
  - He chose that selfless life for the welfare of the nation, India and its people. He believed in it.
- Determination: He was always with a strong determination that he will definitely achieve independence to the nation. He never let the confusion come into his mind in this aspect.
  - He sincerely made his efforts to reach the goal and attain independence.
- Devotion: Mahatma Gandhi with his self-devotion united the determination of the people. Many of them don't have primary education.
  - With his self-less life, he inspired many people and encouraged them to participate in the freedom struggle

- Self-discipline: All the years how was he able to stand on his determination? May be many times he got the opportunities to avail selfish benefits. If others were in his position, they may have been tempted to avail those selfish benefits.
    - But he was never ever tempted to do so. With his strong determination, will-power and '**Self-discipline**', he ultimately brought independence to the nation!

Appearance & Dressing

Time is broadly divided into three parts.

First one is **past**. It is related to memory.

Second is **future**. It is related to our imagination of our hopes and desires.

And the Third is **present**. It is related to 'today'. In this '**today**' **all our opportunities are wrapped up**.

In this 'today', many opportunities are waiting for you. For example, your boss or officer may be thinking to give you a promotion. The interview you are attending may open the doors for you and provide the job that you are seeking. May be the 'progress' is waiting for you in the business you are in with its arms wide...

You should get ready to please the "today'. For that, you have to sit in a chariot connected with the 'manners' as horses, 'self-confidence' as whip, 'appearance' as your weapon and then step into the war field. Automatically, the doors of opportunities will open and make way for you.

Your Dressing Reveals 'What You Are'

The anxiety to change life is seen often in modern days than in the past. In this regard, we can see many self-help books that are widely available in the market like 'Positive Thinking', 'How to improve Self-Confidence', 'How to Rewrite your life', etc...

Even we can observe many Psychologists and Hypnotists giving advertisements in newspapers saying that 'contact us and we change your personality'. These are the efforts to cash the weaknesses of the people...

Nobody can improve the past. But one can always improve the future.

So also, you can't alter your height, but you can always change your appearance.

The people we meet in our daily life assess us by our dressing or appearance. This is called as the first impression....

In order to impress others, we have to be careful with our dressing and appearance.

There are two types of people who don't care about their dressing....

- First – The Rich. There is nothing to prove about their dressing to impress others.
- Second- The Poor. Because of their poverty, they can't afford to dress properly and can't impress others. They can't lose anything.
- The Remaining People – You, me and all of us – To achieve success, we have to impress others through our dressing and appearance.

So a **Dress Code** or rather a decent dress code plays an important role! That's why in big companies and firms, employees have a dress code. For example, gents should be in shirt and wear a tie. Ladies should be with less make up and be with a decent dressing and hairstyle.

Situational Appearances

In the office timings, generally from 9 am to 6 pm, the dressing style of the employees should reflect their image. After office hours, they can dress according to their taste. Women should observe one important aspect because they have to play the role of a wife, mother, sister, daughter, advisor and an employee too! Therefore, the same kind of dressing will not suit for all these roles. So a woman has to dress according to her role! Especially, their simplicity in their dressing always draws more attention towards them.

The success secret lies in knowing how the dressing and appearance impresses others. To know this, it is an art which both the ladies and gents should learn and master.

Life is a Special Occasion

Many of them maintain two types of dressing. **Casual wear** and **Party wear**. Casual wear is for daily wear and Formal wear is for Special Occasions like functions, parties and meetings. But one thing has to be remembered-

Life is a Special Occasion! In today's competitive world, if you don't want to lose any opportunity, your dressing should be polished and balanced.

Your dressing should reveal your economic status, educational status, your honesty, your sophistication, your past and present achievements, your moral character, etc... then only people will be attracted towards you.

Our dressing covers 90 percent of our body. Only 10 percent of our body is reflected. So we should be very careful with our dressing......

You are Selling Yourself

Imagine that you are searching for an employment or an employee. Do you know why the company or the employer has selected you for the post?

- ❑ Because of your honesty
- ❑ Because of your knowledge, education and intelligence

The above-mentioned two qualities are revealed only through your dressing and appearance. Your employer or the company assesses the two qualities in you by looking at your dressing and appearance.

Every year, we come across different models (ladies and gents) projecting different types of cosmetic products in the various advertisements. Crores of money is spent all over the world in the form of advertisements. However, their main objective is to draw or attract the attention and confidence of the customers!

So also, you are like a product in the market. Your external appearance is an advertisement to the product. The companies look at your appearance and try to buy you.

To draw a good income for your knowledge and services, you should project yourself as a precious and expensive person. Primarily, this is possible only with your dressing and appearance.

Don't forget that the persons who want to buy you are experienced and intellectual executives. They will assess you keenly in different aspects before offering you a good amount of income or salary.

So you are painting your personality, your background and your future on the canvas of dressing. There will be only one chance to create a positive impression about you in the minds of others.

As we all know, *the first impression is the best impression!*

Dressing Tips

Neat dressing is an art and following are some of the tips for it:

- The dress you wear should not be too tight or too lose. It should be moderate.
- The dressing should slightly expose your natural, beautiful shapes and at the same time, cover your defects.
- Always wear ironed clothes.
- To be a gentleman, don't wear cheap branded shirts.
- The zip of the trousers should be neat and should not be visible.
- The straps of the bra in ladies should not be exposed as it creates a cheap impression. Never wear a black bra under a white blouse or a see through blouse.
- Never wear a complete black dress, particularly when you attend an interview or a meeting. Black dress reveals violent behaviour, lack of confidence and bad omen.
- Don't wear a very bright colour and big checks on your dresses.
- Ladies can use mild perfume than a strong perfume because it creates a cheap impression.
- Some people use their pockets as dustbins by keeping all sorts of things. It gives a cheap impression.Its better to keep a pen, mobile and your vallet in the case of men.
- A beard suits artists than academicians. If you are used to grow the beard, always trim it.

Clothing Styles

The minute care you take in your style of dressing will create a lot of impact on others. For example:

- **Length of the shirt**: Many of them don't know how to choose the length of their shirts. For them a small advice ÷
  Shirts should always cover the buttocks- there is a formula-
  Measure your height and multiply it with 2 and minus 4 from it. For example, if you are 5 feet 6 inches, it means 66 inches, half of it is 33. Minus 4 from it and the remainder is 29. The length of your shirt should be 29 inches.
- **Shirt collar**: The collar of the shirt should touch the neck. There should not be folds on the shoulders. If you have a round face or a broad face, never wear round collared shirts and wide collared shirts.
  If you have an oval shaped face or a long face, never wear a long-pointed collared shirt.

If you have a short neck, you should not wear collars that cover your neck.

- **Trousers**: Trousers should be of correct fitting. The front side crease should be in the middle of the leg. To know the fitting, whether it's stitched or readymade, wear it, then sit down and get up. If it comes to the actual condition without any protrusion, it's of a correct fitting.
- **Length of the trousers**: The bottom of your trousers should be at the feet and upon the shoes. Socks should not be seen under the trousers.
- **Neck Tie**: Iif you wear a tie, you should wear a suit. Wear only silk ties, because they can be easily knotted. After knotting the tie, it should reach the buckle of your belt. It should not be below it or above it. The colours of the necktie may be Red, Navy Blue, Burgundy or Forest Green, etc according to the suit and shirt.
- **Belt**: The colour of your belt should match with the colour of your shoes.
- **Shoes**: You should not wear white shoes or sandals. When you wear a white dress, you have to wear black shoes. Black shoes suit all dresses and are fit for all times. Always keep your shoes properly polished. The colour of your socks should match or go with the colour of your shoes.
- **Underwear/Undergarments**: Many of us are not careful with their inner wear. Underwear and other undergarments increase the confidence in a person. Moreover, clean and properly fitted undergarments are hygienic as well as make you appear smarter. Torn underwears will subconsciously reduce your self-confidence. So vests, briefs, bras and panties should be neat, proper and comfortable.

What Types of Spectacles Should You Choose?

Generally, people who have a problem with their eyesight use spectacles. Some of them use for fashion. Whatever the reason may be, if they follow some of the following advices regarding spectacles, they may look beautiful:

- The shape of the spectacles should be according to the shape of the nose and face. For example, those who have a long nose should use low-bridged frame. The people with short nose must use a high-bridged frame.
- People with a round face look beautiful in a square frame.
- People with rectangular face should use a round frame.

- People with a long face appear attractive if they use a big frame, straight and thick at the bottom.
- People with a diamond shaped face may use an oval shaped frame.
- People who have a broad forehead with a triangular face should use a lightweight frame with a curve at the bottom.

Colour Chart for Clothing

To know what colour of clothing we should wear, one can follow the tips given below:

- When we grade the clothes from1 to 10, all the light colours are between 1 and 5 and the dark colours are between 5 and 10.
- Of all the light colours, white is considered to be no. 1. Auburn, Navy Blue, Royal Blue, Grey, Charcoal, Black, etc are in between 5 and 10. They are called as classic colours.
- Dark colours make a person look serious. Businesspersons and success achievers wear dark colours. These colours project the image of authority. The persons who wear dark colours usually make a strong imprint on others.

1 to 5 colours in the colour chart, which are of lighter shades are worn during the leisure time or during entertainment activities. They generally look good and decent. So...

The persons who want to look successful should wear dark colours between 5 and 10.

"BE WHAT YOU WANT TO BE."

"Whatever your mind can conceive and believe, your mind can achieve."

— W. Clement Stove

The People who Utilise Time and the People who Misuse their Time

Time is precious, the people who misuse time can't achieve success in their lives. Your attitude towards time and the way you manage it depends upon your attitude towards your life. Now examine yourself whether you are utilising time or misusing it.

People misusing the time	People utilising the time
❍ No goal or aim in life.	❍ There is an aim or goal in life.

❍ They are in between certain situations and unable to tackle them.	❍ They can manage the situations.
❍ They don't have their own ideas and believe the news from the media, and are influenced by it. ❍ They are unable to recognise the opportunities and blame others for their loss and defeat. ❍ Repeatedly commit the blunders and don't learn the lessons. ❍ They are slaves of their own habits. ❍ They have a negative attitude. ❍ Never try to change the situations or conditions that they live in. ❍ Blindly believe the news in the media and think that they know everything but never try to study them in depth. right. ❍ Don't know their weaknesses and defects.	❍ After thorough examination, they believe or accept a new idea or leave an old idea. ❍ They learn lessons from their defeats. ❍ They are with positive attitude ❍ They are confident of achieving success. ❍ To enrich their knowledge and experiences, they meet different persons who have excelled in various fields. ❍ They have a positive attitude. ❍ They know their defects and weaknesses. They put various efforts to set them

Self-Discipline – Mind

(Self-Discipline lesson-3)

Do you know what is mind?

In the box of your mind, there are six rows. If you understand how your mind works in these six rows, then you can understand self-discipline.

First Row – (Ego): This gives you the will power. As the Supreme Court, our Ego governs on the rows of the remaining mind. The 'Ego' has the power to alter or cancel the proposals made by the mind in the remaining rows.

Second Row – (Emotion): The driving force for our thoughts and plans is produced here.

Third Row – (Reason): The thoughts that come out from our emotions and imaginations are assessed and accordingly, the changes in our behaviour are shaped here.

Fourth Row – (Imagination): The methods for the plans and ideas that you wish are produced here.

Fifth Row – (Conscience): Your needs, plans and thoughts, whether they are ethical and justified are assessed here.

Sixth Row - (Memory): All your past experiences and its passions are stored in this row. This row is like a record keeper that reveals various situations of your life. The more linkage between these rows, the more it makes you to carry out self-discipline in your life.

"BE WHAT YOU WANT TO BE."

Success Formula-2

- ❑ You have to set a goal or an aim.
- ❑ Write on a paper clearly as a statement, what you are planning to achieve, that is your goal or aim.
- ❑ To reach your goal, you have to lose some luxuries. Write those things that you have to lose.
- ❑ Immediately, you have to start the work to implement your plan.
- ❑ You have to be careful while implementing the plan so that you do not miss it.
- ❑ If you face failure, review the plan carefully and make slight changes. But don't make the changes only for the failure.
- ❑ While implementing the plan, don't hesitate to take the support of people who are related to it.
- ❑ Be away from the people who are discouraging, dull and with negative thinking. Always be with optimists and elated people.
- ❑ Don't waste a day without implementing the plan. Always be happy and jolly.
- ❑ While achieving your goal, even when you look at it from the farthest distance, never be discouraged but move forward with a hope that one day definitely you can achieve it.
- ❑ Always have a positive mind. Never allow fear, envy, greed, jealousy, mistrust, veng hatred, intolerance and laziness into your mind.

Social Skills

(Pleasing the People)

To be a part of the society, one should not only know how to dress but also know how to please the people. It is also called as 'Positive Behaviour'.

When you look at the success of a person, around 85 percent of it is achieved only through pleasing the people. Pleasing people means being positive to them, getting things done by them effectively, making them to cooperate with you, and likewise achieving your goal....

To please the people, you should know some social skills. Let's discuss in detail how these social skills help us to achieve your goals and please the people:

Your Dressing Should Be Formal

To wear modern and beautiful dress is a part of sophistication. But it shouldn't look like a dress which you cannot wear for a long time, or appear too gorgeous, or very fancy.

Suppose when you attend a party, your dress and makeup shouldn't reveal that you have taken a lot of pain to look like that, instead it should look casual.

Always changing dresses according to the latest fashion trends is also not a good habit and method. It reveals your imitative attitude and lack of stable individuality.

It's also not a good idea to have a number of dresses in your wardrobe. It gives a wrong impression about you that you have an excessive self-love.

So, your dressing should be neat and clean. You should look like a perfectly groomed person.

Never wear gaudy and flashy coloured dresses. Those types of dresses make you look like a silly person. Others also fix their attention on your clothes than on you.

Speak with a Smile

Many people don't smile as they have to. Observe this in your colony, street, office and in your house. They smile less. Even they smile to impress others like switch on and switch off.

According to a survey at a big university, men usually smile 70 percent near women and 12 percent near other men. It means men generally don't want to impress men until or unless he is a higher up or a boss.

Smile has lot of importance in the communication when it takes place between two people. It gives a positive response. If anybody talks with a smiling face, you feel very happy. You also develop fondness and good opinion upon him/her.

A survey at a departmental store revealed that the sales had increased by about 20 percent when the salesperson talked to his customers with a smiling face. Smiles have a lot of importance and definitely make a difference:

- ❑ When you speak to a person with a smiling face, they feel relaxed and respond to you in a positive manner.
- ❑ When you smile, your face looks attractive to others.
- ❑ When you smile unknowingly, happiness enters into your mind. The reason for this is your brain releases some secretions related to happiness!
- ❑ Smile also releases the tension. Surveys reveal that smile or laughter releases more stress than other exercises.

Hence, when there so many advantages with laughter, let's not harm it by neglecting it. So always have a smile or laughter on your face!

A Tranquil Face

A tranquil face means, keeping a calm face without any seriousness. Always have a peaceful or tranquil face with a pleasant smile when you are among other persons. Even in difficult situations, you should have a pleasant face. This is how you can be sophisticated and confident!!

If you are confident even in difficult situations, the people around you will definitely yield to you. They will honour, respect and compliment you. Sometimes, they may be wonderstruck with your attitude.....

Your Voice

To achieve success, not only your appearance and words, but also your voice plays an important role. So while speaking, you have to take care of your voice.

- Don't speak with a loud voice or a very low voice but with a moderate voice so that others can understand your words clearly.
- Speaking with a loud voice indicates your psychological stress and tension, so also the stuttered voice.
- While speaking, stress the important words in the matter and while ending the sentence, reduce your voice.
- Don't speak hastily or slowly.
- While speaking with four or five persons,speak 160 words per minute and when you speak with one or two persons, speak 175 words per minute.
- If you find any defects in your voice, practise some music.

For this, try to listen to the songs of famous singers like S.P. Bala Subramanyam and Janaki. Enjoy their pleasant voice.

Posture

John Robert Powers, many years ago established a modelling firm in America. His main aim was to reveal the charm and poise of models to the ordinary women. So he established a school called 'Powers Finishing and Charm'. He began to train how to behave like a model to the ordinary women.

Do you know what was the first aspect taught in that school??

Posture!!

Posture regarding how to sit, how to stand, how to walk, etc....

If you know the secrets of posture, your dressing will make you to look dignified.

We can learn many things from the military people regarding the postures. When you enter into a room with a gathering in it, immediately the people look at your dress and posture and make an impression about you. This is called as the first impression.

The first impression may be positive or negative. Everything depends upon your body postures. They will continue to have this same impression until they study you completely. So you should be very careful with your body posture.

Body Language

These days many books are available in the market regarding body language. Body language has been given a lot of importance.

Your body movements, head, looks, etc…reveal what you are. Our body language is a part of the body psychology.

Do you know an amazing thing?!!

When we speak with others-

- ❑ We use about 55% of the body language
- ❑ 38% of our tone according to the issue
- ❑ 7% of it is language

By this, we can understand how much importance body language has in communication.

Following are some of the important tips:

- ❑ When you are among others never bite the nails, don't shake your head or legs, and never tap on the chair or table with your fingers. This sort of actions reveal your nervousness to others.
- ❑ Even if you are nervous, try to appear cool and calm. Poise and courage can be learnt through practice.
- ❑ Take care of the laughter when you are with others. Especially ladies!!
- ❑ So also, don't put a stony face.
- ❑ When you speak with a person, look straight into the eyes of that person so that there can be a comfortable conversation.

If you want to learn further about the body language, try to purchase the book, "Body Language" written by the author of this book.

Straight Walking

Straight walk makes you to look dignified. Keep the head up and eyes looking straight ahead. Avoid pushing your head forward. Keep your shoulders properly unified with the rest of your body.

- ❑ Never walk keeping both the hands in the pocket. At least, hands should be seen outside.

Be on Time

To maintain a cordial relation with others, always remember the following things:

- ❑ When you have an appointment at a certain time, try to be there on time.

- If you are late, others may think about you as a careless person. If it becomes a continuous habit, others may lose confidence in you.
- Even they can feel that they are not given importance.
- If you are unable to reach at a particular place on time because of some urgency, inform the matter through phone or by any other means.
- Remember one thing, waiting for a person who never comes on time is the most horrible thing!

Remember the Names

Do you know this is the sweetest and pleasant sound that any person likes to hear from others? To listen his/her name, when it is uttered by others!!

- When you meet persons and develop acquaintance with them, try to remember the names of those persons. Whenever you come across those persons, if you call them with their names, they feel very happy.
- They also develop a liking towards you. This increases your self-confidence and you can win them.

Forgive Minor Mistakes

Some people are very sensitive. They react for over minute issues. This shows their childish mentality. It is good to forgive others for their minute mistakes. Sometimes, mistakes happen unintentionally or due to some unavoidable circumstances.

You must ignore those mistakes. By doing so, you'll not lose anything. You should accept not only the positive qualities of your friends, but also their weaknesses.

Sense of Humour or Seriousness

- If you are able to impress the people around you with your sense of humour, you will be a successful person. If you can't do it, it's good to maintain seriousness.
- Your behaviour should gain you the respect and affection but not contempt.
- The comfort in the seriousness is that others can't read your mind. You can also cover your defects.
- Even people will be scared to speak with serious persons. It's better to maintain silence and seriousness when you don't have a sense of humour!!

No Aggression but only Relaxation

Nobody likes people who are emotional and aggressive. They think that he/she is mentally disbalanced. So don't be overreactive and aggressive. Always think cooly before responding.

Nobody likes to employ people who are too sensitive or aggressive.

You can gain a good image in the minds of other people, if you are calm and balanced.

Don't Talk about Salary and Your Earnings

Never ask about the salary and earnings of others when you are conversing with them.

By chance if the situation demands about these particulars, make up a face that shows disinterest....

Some Personal Details

Listening to others carefully is an art. It's a social skill. Sometimes, you should reveal your personal details. Then only a bond develops between the persons.

In friendship or a relationship, if you don't reveal anything about yourself, others will lose confidence in you and they may not like you.

This can be seen in women particularly. For example:

- ❑ When a woman shares her secrets with other women, they immediately become friends. They also exhibit the same readiness to share their secrets.

In other words, if a woman has more number of friends, we can understand that she is sharing her secrets with them!

But never be like a 'Chatter Box', as people do not like this type of persons because they are too boring.

Live with a Smile and Win with a Smile

When you keep an angry face, around 112 muscles of your face react. But to smile only 13 muscles of your face are enough.

So it is easy to laugh than keeping an angry face!

- ❑ When you look at a person with a smiling face, it says that "I am accepting you without any conditions."
- ❑ Your smiling face makes others feel that they are given importance and value. It also gives an impression that you want to maintain friendliness.

- ❑ Your smile has a lot of impact! There is a proverb in China, "The person who can't smile should not open a shop!"
- ❑ Smile is an important element for the Businessmen. It gains good relationship with others.
- ❑ Smile extracts positive response from others. Even it can erase the negative feelings from the persons who have a negative attitude.
- ❑ Your smile increases your 'self-esteem' and also others' 'self-esteem'.

So always try to live with a smile!!!

Never Spread Rumours

Never talk bad about others or spread rumours.

Some people always talk about others, as they are villains. This type of talk reveals your bad manners. People are generally not very friendly with such type of persons.

Remember, your rudeness or bad manners make the people to dislike you!

Give Importance/Recognition to Others

By giving an honest recognition to others, you are increasing their self-esteem.

What is recognition??

In every person, there is a good quality. It may be big or small. For example: He/She may be beautiful or creative or honest or a good speaker…

Try to identify that quality and compliment it. He/She feels proud of that compliment and this enhances his/her self-esteem.

This will also be good for you because the others will value your words. They will feel comfortable and secured in your company.

Behave Politely

When you behave with others, as they are also prominent persons giving weightage to their words, they will feel really happy.

Giving prominence to others means – paying attention to people, or to listen to them carefully.

Even if you are not interested, if you ask questions in the middle of the conversation, they may feel that you are giving importance to them and that will be eventually be favourable to you.

Never Pass Unnecessary Comments or Remarks

Some people always boast about themselves and criticise others. Especially, they pass disgraceful comments about the low caste people and the poor.

These comments reveal your narrowmindedness and your snobbery.

- Try to understand that there are diversities among the people like different opinions, lifestyle, customs, traditions, etc...Even if you don't like these diversities, you have no right to mock at them.
- If don't like their lifestyle or their likes, hide those comments in your mind itself. By doing so, you will look sophisticated and others will respect you.

Gracious Departing

When you are among other people, never try to be the last person to depart. It does not look good.

When you finish the talk and observe that the topic is diverting towards gossip, try to change the topic or depart from that place.

By doing so you will not 'miss' anything but your exit, you will definitely make others feel that they are 'missing' you. This is what gracious departing means!!

It needs courage to depart when you are deeply immersed in a conversation with others. It all depends on your considerate time sense.

Others should also feel that you are not happy about your going away in the middle of the conversation and they should feel your absence.

Behaviour with Waiters

When you go to a hotel or a restaurant, your behaviour should be charming with the waiters. If you do so, then whenever you go there, they will respect you. Even they may show you a good table.

- Never shout at the waiters or don't cut jokes with them. Don't ignore their presence and speak secrets in front of them.
- Give the sufficient tip to the waiters but don't give them too much money as a tip. If you have any complaint against a waiter, you should politely ask the manager to meet you, but never try to quarrel with the waiter directly and lower your position.

Friendship with Persons Having Positive Attitude

You should be very careful and selective when you make friends and companions. Long time companionship with any person makes you to get attracted towards their thoughts, opinions and principles. It is not only important to have or inculcate positive thoughts, participate in positive conversation, it is also very important to make friendship with the persons of positive attitude.

- ❑ Positive people will always inspire us. They make us to move ahead. They bring out the potentialities that are placed or hidden within us.
- ❑ Persons with a negative attitude always speak about their sorrows, sufferings and their complaints. They complain us about the ill-treatment of the world, misunderstanding between the partners, the harassment of the boss, etc... and bother us.
- ❑ Try to be far away from these types of persons. Always be with persons who make you cheerful, bring out your capabilities and encourage your talents.

Remember

The persons with whom we live together will greatly influence our lives. So we should be very careful while choosing them.......

"BE WHAT YOU WANT TO BE."

Win with Your Words!

(Your words should be like magical arrows!)

Communication plays an important role to build up relationships with others. We communicate with others to share our emotions, thoughts and opinions. To get recognition in the society or to maintain friendly relations, one should know what to speak and what not to speak in different situations and in different contexts.

This is called as "wise speaking."

Some of the techniques regarding good and ideal speaking:

Your Words Reveal Your Secrets

Have you ever heard A.B.Vajpayee's speech? You will be mesmerised with his speech. After listening to it, you will be compelled to say, "How nicely he spoke!"

So also, while you speak, you should be careful with your language and attitude. It should impress others!

- ❑ While speaking your voice should be confident and pleasant. It should sound as if you are controlled and a positive attitude person. Your conversation may be personal or official, but you must remember three vital aspects while speaking:
- ❑ Never search for words
- ❑ Never boast about yourself and listen to others.
- ❑ Speak according to the situation. This also called as 'timing'.
- ❑ When others are speaking, you nod your head to say, 'yes' or 'no'. So also some people while speaking nod their heads, and giggle, it's not good.

- During the conversation, keep a pleasant face without shaking the head. It can be acquired through practice.
- Some people always interfere in the middle and want to tell their opinion, when the other person is conversing. With this interruption, other person feels embarrassed. It reveals your lack of manners.
- Always you should be polite while conversing with others. Never open your voice until the person stops speaking.
- When you speak to a person look into his face. But not always look into his eyes.
- Never ask 'personal' questions, when they are not willing to tell.
- Never talk about cost and expenses.
- Never cut cheap jokes feeling that you are an expertise.
- Never beat around the bush.
- Never point out the mistakes of others when they speak.
- Never talk low about the achievements of others. It reveals your contempt.
- Never talk with a loud voice
- Never boast about your capabilities and talents.

Never Let Your Feelings to Others

Some people are like an open book. They can't hide anything from others and reveal every personal detail. They will let their reactions through their face, voice, eyes and body. We call these persons as 'open-hearted' or 'frank'.

Everyone in the society wants to use these types of openhearted persons. Sometimes by knowing what you are, people try to manipulate you.

The surroundings you grow, pampering of the parents and insecurities that build up in your mind are the reasons to develop open heartedness.

Every person has problems and insecurities in more or less ration. You have to receive them as challenges. Man's perfections is revealed through overcoming those situations.

When you observe many persons around you, they can't sit or stand stable for one minute. They move their hands and legs, shake their heads. These gestures reveal your nervousness.

Have you ever observed this kind of nervousness in you? Have you ever thought that whether you are also behaving in the same manner in front of others?

In order to get recognition in the society, firstly, you should learn to be relaxed without any movements. It is very difficult to keep the body in a relaxed form. But through practice, you can achieve it. A relaxed body has poise. By this, your self-confidence and individuality is revealed to others. Individuality makes you a wonderful person.

Never Impose Your Ideas on Others

In day to day conversations, some people always want to take an upper hand over others. They feel what ever they say is correct. They can't accept others words.

When there is a strong point in others talk, try to listen to it carefully. By doing so, you can get an opportunity to broaden your opinions and study others. Even when there is no point in other's talks, give a confident smile and change the topic on other subject.

Losing a friend by winning an argument is not at all virtuous.

Listening is an Art

Many times because of many reasons, we receive other's words in different forms. The reason for it is, lack of concentration, not listening carefully and because of a bad mood. This leads to 'gossips'.

In English, generally we speak 125 words per minute. However, we think four times before we speak. It means, we think 500 words in a minute. When a person speaks, our brain receives 125 words and still has a free time to think of about 375 words. While listening to a person we use that free time to think of 375 words on an interesting topic. These thoughts influences what we listen and change the meaning by the time it reaches to our brain. We have two ears and one tongue, so we have to listen more than to speak.

Speak Less and Listen More

Follow the rules mentioned below while speaking with others:

- ❑ Listen to others with concentration
- ❑ If you are in a stress, first keep aside your stress and then listen
- ❑ Don't misinterpret others words with your thoughts, beliefs and prejudice.
- ❑ Never interrupt in the middle, when others are speaking. Wait until they complete it.
- ❑ While listening never divert your thoughts on others matters
- ❑ Observe the body language of others while listening to them

To achieve success in life, one has to remember this maxim:

Speech is Silver, Silence is Gold.

Everybody Likes Self-Praise

It is human tendency that we are more concerned about ourselves than in others, in many aspects of our life, such as:

- We have our own ideas, experiences, emotions, arrogance and anxieties.
- But we should not forget that others also have same ideas, experiences, emotions, arrogance, anxieties etc.. Like us.
- To maintain positive communication with others we should show interest in others. That interest should be exhibited honestly.
- Communication is a two-way situation. One will speak and the other will listen.
- You have to draw the attention of others to make them listen to you.
- To draw the attention and concentration of others towards yourself, you have to choose the things that create interest in them.

Do you know generally what people are interested to speak in the first place?

Self-Boasting and Pride

- People like to speak about their interests, hobbies and their thoughts. Generally women like to speak about their home, cooking, children etc.. Men like to speak about cricket, stock market, politics etc…

So by choosing the topics according to the person's interest you can please them.

The second aspect people like to speak: **To speak about their opinions!**

- Sometimes even when you can't agree with others opinion, to get your task done or to remain your friendship you have to accept with their opinion patiently. Don't argue with them.

Losing an argument is better than losing a friend.

The third aspect people like to speak: **To speak about others!**

- Everyone likes to take some pleasure by speaking something about others. This type of talk is called as gossip or rumor. There is no basis for such type of gossip. Generally while talking about others people like to speak only bad points of those persons.

In such situations, you try to bring out good qualities and positive points of that person about whom you are talking. By doing so, you can have a pleasant and positive level conversation.

The fourth aspect people like to speak: **To speak about what is happening around the world!**

- ❑ Some people have lot of knowledge and information on some particular issues. By listening to them carefully, you can also increase your knowledge and broaden your thinking.

The fifth and the last aspect people like to speak: **To speak about you!**

- ❑ They will prefer least to listen about you. But they don't like to listen your negative aspects or your sorrows and sufferings. So try to concentrate on the other persons talk. After listening whatever he says then talk about you.

So first let him speak, later tell him about you......

Speak Positively

Positive speaking works like a magical power. Negative speaking keeps away.

Suppose you are not feeling well or suffering from some sickness. So whenever a person comes to you or whenever you meet a person if you complain about your sickness, you can draw their attention and sympathy but it's a temporary one. They think of you as a 'pain symbol'.

Here the author of this book remembers a friend's saying:

"Never let your sorrows, quarrels and sufferings to anybody. Half of the people will not care them. Other half of the people will feel happy for your sorrows, quarrels and sufferings".

Behave as If You are Impressed by Others

- ❑ While conversing with other person, if you behave as if you are impressed by his talk he feels very happy.
- ❑ Impressed behaviour means keeping your complete attention on the other person's talk.
- ❑ When you talk less about you, the other person feels that he is given more prominence. You have to behave as if you are fascinated with his life and other aspects. Be careful, no over action.
- ❑ Nobody likes to listen about your intelligence, knowledge, achievements etc....
- ❑ Instead, by remembering other person's interests and emotions if you speak accordingly he will think that you are an intelligent person and interesting person.

- It's a fact that others will not listen 80% of what we say. They like to listen about themselves, so ask them about their goals, interests, opinions, experiences.....
- By asking these type of questions you can have their complete attention, wait for the time and reveal your need to them.

In other words even if you speak with a fool as if he was like a "great person" he will try to become close and surrender to you...

Wait Until You Get the Chance to Speak

Nobody can continuously speak. A time comes when one , to stops speaking. Then you can speak about yourself, but until then you have to wait patiently....

While speaking about yourself, speak little so that it does not bore others yourself!

Conversation with Strangers

Till now, whatever we have discussed is about our friends and acquaintances. Now, you have to speak with a stranger, do the following:

Suppose you attend a party or function and many of them are strangers to you. You feel lonely and stand aside watching others speaking happily,

How do you behave in such situation?

How do you develop friendship with them?

The best thing is first you take the initiative and begin a conversation.

Choose a person, who is lonely and go to him/her directly. Go with a positive attitude that he/she will be friendly with you, but never have a negative attitude (Generally, in such situations everyone respond spositively).

Have a general talk. Never try to speak philosophy or serious talk to reveal your intelligence. Start talking about you, but very less so that the other person feels relaxed in your company. Then ask questions about him. Meanwhile, the anxiety between you and him will melt and then have a good conversation....

An Advice

When you are among a group of persons and if you know when to open your mouth and when to close it, you have won half of the world!!

Best Speaking Means....

Dale Carnegie, a popular American writer, once wrote, "How to win friends and influence people" and other books on self-help. Once he attended a party in New York. There he was introduced to a rich woman, who visited Africa and had come back. Immediately she said, "Oh, Mr. Carnegie, I heard a lot about you. Is it true that you are the best speaker in the New York City?"

Carnegie answered, "Thank you very much Madam! I heard that you visited Africa, what made you to go there?"

She told the reason for visiting Africa. Again, Dale Carnegie asked,

"Whom have you taken with you to Africa?", "when did you come from Africa?", "what did you do in Africa?", "where did you stay?", "what places have you seen in Africa?" etc....

They conversed for about 20 minutes in the party and in that 20 minutes, she spent 95 percent of her time giving answers to his questions.

Next day in a newspaper, she has given a statement that "It's true, Mr. Carnegie is the best speaker in the New York City."

So what do you understand from this??

Best Speaking Means- To Speak Less than Others

You have to please others. You have to behave as if you are attentive to their talks. Appreciate them by saying, "thank you" whenever the time demands. Praise their achievements, qualities and actions accordingly.

The questions like, What? Where? When? How? Who? Why? will encourage others to speak out....

Self-Discipline Lesson-4

To Keep your Thoughts Rhythmic

Your mind is filled with many thoughts, images, emotions and the past memories that you saw, heard and learnt, your knowledge, the impressions of your joys and sorrows,etc. All these things influence your talk, walk and your behaviour.

All your thoughts, images, emotions, memories, knowledge, the impressions of your joys and sorrows are like various musicians playing their own tunes. There is no harmony among the tunes. Imagine how it would be when you enter into a room listening to different tunes without any synchronisation....

Suppose, if a director makes them to sit in an order and make them to play all the instruments rhythmically, wouldn't it be melodious to listen?

So what should be your duty?

In order to control, mould your life and your future according to your wishes- you have to become the musical director of your mind.

You have to conduct an orchestra with the musical instruments of your mind like your thoughts, emotions, images, memories and impressions of joys and sorrows by maintaining harmony among them.

You have to mould your life to play a beautiful and melodious music.

This is what self-discipline means!

Don't Be Nervous

In the world we live in, some people always look nervous. Some people look nervous only in some situations. Some people always look quite like Gautam Buddha's disciple.

Biting the nails, patting the nose and touching the lips with the tongue are some of the qualities of nervousness.

Generally, we feel nervous when there is an anxiety or mental stress.

To attend an interview, to speak with strangers, to enter into the room of a strict officer, to write an exam, to deliver a lecture on the stage in front of others, or proposing love to your girl friend for the first time are some of the situations that cause nervousness in young men.

When we are nervous, often our fingers move towards the face, head and neck. Especially, they move towards the direction of the defects of our bodies. These things are done unknowingly.

For example, if a person feels that his hair is falling down, when he is in anxiety, unknowingly puts his fingers over his hair. A person who feels that he is balding, when he is nervous sets his hair in the balding portion.

So also, if a person has a mark on his cheek, when talking to his girlfriend, if he feels nervous he touches that mark unknowingly.

To touch the beard, to pat the eyebrows, to pull down the earrings with the thumb and forefinger are some of the things that are done when a person is nervous. These are called as Auto-contacts.

The persons make 'Auto-contacts' to console themselves or to reduce their tensions which is built up in their minds.

The main reason for nervousness is lack of self-confidence in a person. Fear and inferiority complex are the reasons for the lack of self-confidence.

If You Walk with Fear, You will Lose ...

The fear that you can't impress a person, the fear that you can't be successful at the interview, the fear that your girl friend rejects your proposal, the fear that your words can be misunderstood by others... all these fears make a person to feel nervous.

Fear, inferiority complex and lack of self-confidence usually occurs in a person who has a negative attitude. Regarding negative attitude, you can read in detail in another chapter of this same book.

Fear breaks the confidence of a person. It also destroys his performance. It makes a person to take a back step. It throws him into the failures.

No person is fearful by birth. But the circumstances and experiences make him fearful. There are chances to control these fears.

To control the fear, first you have to understand that you are fearful. You have to accept it!

To remind you of the fear, some warning signals emerge by destroying your performance. You have to find out those warning signals. They are like this....

Self-Talk

"Why did I do like this?"

"I should have done this work!"

"If I have ??"

When we are fearful, we , generally do this self-talk.

Self- talk reveals our fear and lack of self-confidence. It is also a warning signal. Self-talk is generally a negative talk.

Suppose a young man attends an interview. Because of some reason, which is not under his control, he comes late. He sits in the waiting room eagerly waiting for the call. During that time, he makes the following thoughts or self-talk.

"I have come late, they will get a bad impression on me, whether I will be selected or not...."

"It's my fault, it's been better if I would have started a little bit early...."

"No use, I will not get this job, as I came late to the interview..."

We talk like this in a negative manner when we are nervous.

Even our body responds in a negative manner and this is called as Body-Talk.

Body-Talk

When we are fearful or nervous, the following change or changes take place in our body:

- ❑ Neck pain
- ❑ Muscles of the shoulder and chest shrink
- ❑ Jaw muscles shrink
- ❑ Swift heartbeat
- ❑ Back pain
- ❑ Mouth becomes dry
- ❑ Drowsiness
- ❑ To sigh deeply
- ❑ Knee shake
- ❑ Laziness
- ❑ Short temper
- ❑ Restlessly moving to and fro, etc...

Many people think that they can overcome nervousness through positive attitude. But it may not always be possible. While making the positive thoughts, negative thoughts will also arise and both will clash.

For example, Let us take the above-mentioned incident.

Your positive thought may say –

"Get relaxed! You fulfil all the requirements that are essential for this job, so definitely you will be selected."

Moreover, at the same time, your negative thought will say-

"You have all requirements! But what happens if anybody with higher qualification comes?? Or what happens, if anybody comes with a big recommendation??"

When we look at the solutions…

Breathing Exercise

- ❑ Take a deep breath, stop it for some time and later slowly release the breath completely.
- ❑ While inhaling the breath, your stomach should rise up like a tide and while exhaling, your stomach should go back.

- Inhaling, stopping and exhaling should be in 1:4:2 ratios. It means if you inhale for 4 seconds, you should stop it for 16 seconds and exhale it for 8 seconds.
- If you do this breathing exercise 4 to 5 times, your body relaxes and you'll get back your lost strength.(You can do this exercise even when you are accompanied by others without their knowledge.)
- When the body relaxes, you have to remember the situation where you felt nervous. Not only this situation, but also, you can remember any other similar situation.
- You have to remember that whole situation like a movie reel and how you behaved, faced and overcame it.
- For example: Let's take the interview incident, you must have faced the same situation previously. Remember your initial schooldays, where you met your headmaster or teacher step by step.
- Entering into the headmaster's room with shivering legs, your answers to his questions.... running out of his room, etc....
- If you remember this whole situation, the fear of facing interview will reduce.
- By remembering the tensed situations in the past and if the same situations repeat in the future, you have to rehearse how to face those situations. These things will help you to overcome your fear and nervousness.

Always Ask Yourself the Following Questions:

- "Why do I fear so much? What happens if I fail in the interview?? I won't get this Job! Let it be I will attend another interview...." These are my trails to get the job. So I have to get on step by step, at any step, I will get the Job....."
- "I can get this job in the first instance, if I attend it without any tension....."
- "Even if I fail in this interview, the biggest loss is not getting the job! But this interview gives me an experience, what to do and what not to do.... So by attending this interview, I am not losing anything, even failure is teaching me some experience....."
- By philosophising like this, your mind becomes stable.
- These things will help you to face any type of situation confidently without any fear or anxiety.

Breathing exercise should be done before facing the above mentioned situations.

Remembering the past incidents and philosophising the failures should be done daily in the morning……

Take it Easy

To overcome nervousness, follow the tips mentioned below:

- First you have to identify your fear through these warning signals:
  - Through your Self-Talk
  - Through your Body-Talk
- After identifying the warning signals, take a deep breath (4 seconds). Stop it for some time (16seconds) and later slowly exhale the breath (8 seconds).
- There is no particular timing to do breathing exercise but while doing it, you have to follow the ratio of 1:4:2.
- You have to calculate the loss if you participate in that situation. By doing so, you will have a stable mind. This experience will also help you as a guideline.

If you follow all the above mentioned principles systematically, you can acquire a new vigour and confidence and face even the nervous situations courageously.

Make Your Style Different!

(Ten Commandments!)

To get a special *recognition or identity in the society, you need a style.* In this competitive world, your style will be an additional qualification and will help you to get recognition.

Your style will help to give a special opinion to others. Your style can be seen in your behaviour, dress, make up, etc...

Observe the actors like Raj Kapoor, Dev Anand, Dilip Kumar, Rajesh Khanna and Amitabh Bachchan in old movies. They had their own special get ups.

While going to a movie, we think of that movie to be like this or that, the mannerisms of the actor to be like this or that, etc... This is because of the style of those actors.

Every actor tries to hide his/her defects and follow a style to highlight his/her merits. For example:

- Amitabh Bachchan has a long neck and to cover this defect, he used is to grow long hair,. so also to cover his long back, he used to tuck in his shirt.
- Rajesh Khanna had a fat butt like ladies. To cover it, he used to wear long shirts or coats.
- Dev Anand had one short leg and a long leg. To cover this, he used to maintain a mannerism in his walk.
    - So also, every actor chose their roles according to their personality, exhibit their mannerisms and set them as their style. For example:

- Aamir Khan is short, so he chooses the roles of a schoolboy, college youth, lover boy, etc.
- Akshay Kumar is tall and has a beautiful physique. He is also well trained in martial arts. So he performs actions by exposing his bare chest and semi- nude body. This is his style.
- So all the actors, according to their bodies and characters exhibit their style, mannerisms, etc. This their success secret!!
    - Even in your real life, you have to set a style according to your personality. It may be through your dress, or behaviour...
- Politicians usually wear a khadi dress or are in white dress.
- Industrialists wear bright coloured suits.
- Movie artists wear colourful shirts.
- Workers wear khakis....

In this manner, people belonging to different occupations have different styles. So also, you have to set a particular style for yourself.

It can be your dress, walk or posture, talking style, etc.....

He or She looks trim in a particular way, he has particular body movements, his convictions and moral values are in a particular manner, his response will be in a particular way, like this way people have to think about you.

The following aspects should reflect your character....

- Your dress style should hide your defects and set to your lifestyle.
- Your behavioural style should be according to your social background.
- The style of your moral values should be according to the principles of the society.
- You will get identity in this competitive world if you maintain a unique style, exclusively yours. Then only, you can impress othersS.
- Then only you will get recognition in your profession and in your social circle. Everybody will talk about-"His style is different!"

Through your style, you'll get popularity.

- In order to get popularity with your style, you have to follow these ten commandments:
    1. You should have confidence in you.
    2. You should know your limitations and accordingly, set your plans.

3. You should have a role model, in his path you have to set your individuality.
4. Eat moderately.
5. You should be ready to appreciate and accept the good qualities of others.
6. You should always examine your efforts and continue the tempo.
7. You should share your happiness and sorrows with your family members, friends and well- wishers.
8. Do some freehand exercises daily, at least for some time.
9. 9. Daily meditate for some time and get relaxed.
10. Examine your faults, mistakes and failures and put your efforts, not to repeat them again.

Your Self-Esteem

The main factor to achieve success is self-esteem.

Acceptance of ourselves for who and what we are at any given time in our lives is called as self-esteem. Self-esteem is the measure for your emotional fitness.

To examine your self-esteem, just answer the following questions:

These questions are general questions. They can't give complete information regarding your self-esteem. But they will help you to think about your self-image and to know your overall attitude towards the life.

Question: How much success you achieved in your life?

Answer: (a) I feel proud of my achievements.

(b) I achieved success in some prominent aspects.

(c) I underwent many failures in all my efforts.

Your confidence and capabilities depend upon the success you achieved in the past. If you underwent failures in the past, by this time you might have lost your confidence.

It's time to increase your self-confidence, so read this entire book carefully.

Question: What is your opinion regarding your appearance?

Answer: (a) I don't like to change my appearance, I like my appearance.

(b) I don't look good at photographs.

(c) It will be good if some of my body parts looked better.

To feel that you should look different, or to be like others reveals your low self-esteem. Try to improve your self-image.

Question: Does your personality attract others?

Answer: (a) Generally, everybody likes me.

(b) It will be nice if I get more recognition among others.

(c) I feel that nobody likes me.

The above answers reveal your actual self-esteem.

The opinion you have towards yourself is the real measure of your self-esteem. So if you have any negative opinions towards, yourself try to forget them!

Question: Do you have any repentance regarding the past incidents?

Answer: (a) Once again, if I get chance of leading this life from the beginning, I will continue to live in the same manner.

(b) I have taken many wrong decisions in the past.

(c) Today, I feel shy for what I have done in the past.

The above answers reflect your self-confidence as well as your self-esteem.

Many people do not think about the past. If you think too much about the faults done in the past, you are destroying your own self-esteem. You can't change what has/had happened in the past, so never regret.

Question: Do you feel that you are performing a prominent role in home and outside the society?

Answer: (a) I feel content with what I do.

(b) I am unable to get appreciation from others.

(c) I am unable to do even a single task.

What do the above answers indicate?

To feel that you are unable to do anything, and that others are unable to accept your task, reveal your inferiority complex. You have to learn many positive steps to increase your self-esteem.

Question: How do you take criticism?

Answer: (a) I like positive criticism because it will help me to mould myself and better myself.

(b) I feel annoyed if anybody criticises me.

(c) I don't like to reveal my opinion thinking that others will criticise me.

The above answers also indicate your self-esteem and thought processes.

Unable to face or accept criticisms reveal your insecure feeling and lack of self-confidence.

Try to enhance your self-esteem by looking at the good qualities in you!

Enhancing Your Self-Esteem

Anybody who has undergone plenty of sorrows and sufferings in his/her life, always finds some good situations or some good qualities to cherish in oneself.

By following the below mentioned aspects, you can boost up your 'Ego' to some extent.

- Write all your positive qualities as a list.
- Recollect the things you achieved in the past and think positively about you.
- Try to set right your defects one by one.
- Set some goals in front of you and try to achieve them one by one.
- Choose an ideal person, try to imitate and live like him. Your choice should be realistic and good.
- Never worry about your faults and failures of the past.
- Never become a drunkard or a drug addict to enjoy artificial importance and sympathy.

SECTION - III
SUCCESS MANAGEMENT

Goal Setting

The Important Aspects to Achieve Success are:

1. Goal setting
2. Appropriate planning to reach that goal

If you show your ability and skill in these two above-mentioned aspects, surely you can achieve success. Goal setting and appropriate planning are the first stepping-stones to achieve success. These two aspects are equal to success. The other efforts you make to achieve success are like commentaries to these two above-mentioned aspects.

The remaining chapters in this book are also like commentaries for this chapter....

Goals As Your Fuels

Goals are like fuels that light the fire of achievements.

The person without goals is like a ship travelling in the sea without compass going in different directions and facing the problems.

With the help of the map and compass, the captain of the ship moves the ship in a straight way towards the shore and reaches safely.

A person who leads a normal life without any achievements or goals can't be happy or contented even if he has all the comforts. Life seems dull to him.

-It is a surprising quality in man!

So every person need some goals.

"What you are today", and in what position you are in today – everything depends upon your thoughts, your actions and your behaviour.

No power in this world will stop you without achieving your goals unless you have a burning desire!

Success Mechanism

In every person, there are two types of mechanisms. They are:

- ❑ First - Success Mechanism
- ❑ Second- Failure Mechanism

Of the above two aspects, failure mechanism is stronger.

Failure mechanism gives importance to temporary pleasures or comforts. It will not show any seriousness in achieving permanent pleasures.

In every person, this failure mechanism works twenty-four hours automatically. This is the reason why many persons show their interest on temporary pleasures than concentrating on permanent pleasures. Success mechanism is different and it needs a goal. To press the trigger of the success mechanism pistol, it needs a goal as a forefinger.

Two persons who are equal in their education, intelligence, experience and social background try to achieve success with the same goal, who do you think will win in such a situation??

The person who has a burning desire will definitely win! So there is a close relationship between achieving the goal and 'desire' towards the goal!

To Pay the Penalty....

H.L. Hunt, one of the world's largest and reputed wealthiest person in America says like this:

"Decide what you want, decide what you are willing to exchange for it. Establish your priorities and go to work." Many people even if they know what they want, they can't achieve it because they don't know what they have to do to achieve it!

There are two facts related to the exchange or penalty you have to pay for achieving the success:

- ❑ First - you have to pay the penalty completely in order to achieve your wish! To pluck the fruits first you have to sow the seeds. It takes a long time to germinate and grow as trees and give fruit. Until then you have to wait patiently! So it is....
- ❑ Second – sometimes that complete penalty has to be paid initially as an advance! Success is not like a restaurant where you pay the bill after eating what all you want to eat. To achieve success you have to pay the complete penalty as an advance second to second

according to the need! The life you are enjoying today is the result for what you have paid in the past. So also the life you enjoy in the future will also depends upon the price you pay today!

Comfort Zone

The main obstacle that stands as a hindrance to achieve success is your comfort zone. This comfort zone keeps the man away from change. Even if it is a positive change....

In order to achieve success we have to accept the change. But the comfort zone in the person opposes the change, because of it the person remains same without achieving any success.

Many of us don't know one thing-

Everybody in this world strives for success. Some will try hard for their success and some will strive for others success.

If you remain in same position without achieving any success in your life, it doesn't mean that you are not striving for the success. Already you might have made efforts but it is for your boss or somebody!

It is better to endeavor for your success than co-operating with others for their success. Isn't it?! Just think......

The goals you want to achieve should be transparent, accurate and specific. Then it will be easier for you to achieve them.

When there are many uses with the goals, many of us will not set the goals!

Reasons for Not Setting the Goals....

There are seven primary reasons for a man for not setting the goals.

It is necessary to know those seven reasons and examine yourself to find whichever reason is applicable to you.

- **First reason- Not Taking the Goals Seriously:** Some people want to have a better and successful life but never try to put the efforts to achieve it. They speak more and work less. They don't have burning desire to lead their life in a more exciting and better way. So don't speak about what you want to do instead show it through your deeds. This is what seriousness means!
- **Second reason- Not Taking up the Responsibilities of Life**: The person who will not accept that he is responsible for his life is equal to a person who buys lottery tickets and then goes home, sits in front of the T.V and wastes his time. They will not set any

goals or plans and simply pass the time like a wayward person. You can read more about this aspect in another chapter.

- **Third reason - Feeling Guilty That They are Fit for Nothing**: The persons who feel inferior about themselves psychologically and emotionally lack self-confidence. Their pessimism makes them afraid to make plans about the future.

  "I can't do this task"

  "There is no use with this planning" etc..

  These types of pessimistic thoughts wipe out the ability of serious planning regarding the goals.

- **Fourth reason – Not Knowing the Importance of the Goals**:

  Some persons are nurtured in the families where the parents don't have any goals. Even they haven't heard their parents talking about "we have to achieve this", "we have to earn this" etc. The persons who are born and brought up in such families where there are no aspirations or ambitions, don't know the importance of those aspects. So they lead a normal life without any goals. The sad part is that about 80 percent of the people around us lead their life without any goals, aspirations, ambitions, ideals etc...

  If they learn to set the goals and proper planning to fulfill their aspirations and ambitions then they can better their life.

- **Fifth reason - Not Knowing how to Achieve the Goals**: From childhood to a particular age say18 to 21, we study in schools and colleges and take a degree.

  But in all these years of our education we are not aware of our goals and plans. Even the teachers or the persons who set the university curriculum are not concerned with these aspects.

  As a result, today we see many educated persons leading an idle life in the society without any employment. The persons who know how to set their goals and plans will be happy, rich and shine in the society.

- **Sixth reason – Fear of Criticisms**: Suppose you belong to a middle class family and daily go to your school on a bicycle. One day if you say to them "when I grow big I'll become rich and travel only in cars", they make fun of you by saying "he is day dreaming".

  Suppose you are a jobless person who is roaming on the roads and sometimes enacting some stage shows. If you say to your friends or family members that "look at me one day I'll become a hero. Either Raghavendra Rao or E.V.V Satyanaryana or S.V. Krishan Reddy will give a chance as a hero", they look at you sympathetically and think that you are a 'fool'.

From our childhood, we are nurtured with these types of comments and criticisms. These things will suppress our aspirations and ambitions.

Parents criticise us in order to make us strong and bold even in adverse situations that are faced in the future. Friends criticize us because they think that we are talking about the impossible things.

All these comments and criticisms of our childhood influence our attitude and later as we grow develop a fear complex in us when we want to set the goals.

When we look at different persons who have excelled in different fields and reached high positions have undergone through these same comments in their childhood.

So never stop to set goals with a fear that you have to face comments and criticisms.

So also, try to encourage others who fear to set goals. Your encouragement to others will motivate you. So use every opportunity to encourage others!!

- **Seventh reason- Fear of failures**: The main hindrance that stands between you and success is the Fear of failure. It will lead you into comfort zone.

This attitude is expressed by saying "I can't do it", "I can't do it".

Many of them don't know the role of failure. The main principle behind it is –

Failures are the Stepping Stones to Success, and it's Impossible to Achieve Success without Failures!!

So failure is a pre-requisite to success.The most successful things in the world are achieved only through failures!

Here Let's Discuss An Example: We all know about Thomas Alva Edison who is the most prolific inventor in history, holding 1,093 US patents in his name, as well as many patents in the United Kingdom, France and Germany. He is credited with numerous inventions that contributed to mass communication and, in particular, telecommunications. These included a stock ticker, a mechanical vote recorder and a battery for an electric car, electrical power, recorded music and motion pictures.

Thomas Edison failed thousands of times before he revolutionized the world by inventing and patenting the incandescent light bulb, because of his desire to create the incandescent light. There is a common story that circulates about "Success and Failure". It has been reported that Edison failed over 5,000 times before perfecting the first electric light bulb. On one occasion, a young journalist challenged Edison saying to him, "Mr. Edison, why do you keep trying to make light by using electricity when you have failed so many times? Don't you know that gas lights are with us to stay?"

To this, Edison replied, "Young man, don't you realise that I have not failed but have successfully discovered six thousand ways that won't work!"

So failure is like a signpost that guides you in correct direction.

Some Principles in Goal Setting

For any person to achieve maximum achievements, he has to follow five basic principles while setting the goals.

- **First - Goals should be according to your character**

  In order to show your 'Best' your goals should project your values and character. 'Values' means the thoughts and beliefs of your mind regarding the aspects, what is correct, what is wrong, what is good, what is bad, what is important and what is nonsense.

  If your values and goals together hand in hand with harmony, you will have high self-esteem. You can also perform your best capabilities.

- **Second – Goals should be according to your talents**

  Every person has talents in some aspects according to his ability and taste. So you have to identify in which aspect you can prove your talent and in which aspect you can display your excellence and try to develop those aspects.

  Without knowing your mind's desire you can't be happy. So first, try to identify your desire..

- **Third – Opportunities can be developed anytime**

  (Read the story of Acres of Diamonds) "Acres of Diamonds" originated as a speech that Conwell delivered over 6,000 times around the world. The John Y. Huber Company of Philadelphia first published it in 1890.

The central idea of the work is that one need not look elsewhere for opportunity, achievement, or fortune—the resources to achieve all good things are present in one's own community. This theme is developed by an introductory anecdote, told to Conwell by an Arab guide, about a man who wanted to find diamonds so badly that he sold his property and went off in futile search for them, the new owner of his home discovered that a rich diamond mine was located right there on the property. Conwell elaborates on the theme through examples of success, genius, service, or other virtues involving ordinary Americans contemporary to his audience: "dig in your own back-yard!"

So opportunities are always in front of you. Your talent and abilities lies in identifying them. It's your duty to recognize them.

- **Fourth - Corresponding**

To bring out the 'Best' in you, you have to set the below-mentioned aspects as your goals. Then you can lead a successful and peaceful life.

- Goals regarding your family and personal life.
- Goals regarding your body and health.
- Psychological and Intellectual goals (goals regarding your education and personality development)
- Goals regarding your career and profession
- Your Economical goals
- Your Spiritual goals (related to your mental peace)

To achieve balance, choose two or three sub-goals for each of the above- mentioned aspects.

By following these things regularly, you can progress in your life achieving success.

- **Fifth - Deciding the main aim of your life**

You can frame many sub-goals. But of all those goals, you have to know the most important goal in your life - The main ambition of your life.

- First analyse all the sub-goals and question like this-

  "Of all these goals, which goal will lead me to achieve all the other goals?"

  That goal may be related to your Business or earning profits. Sometimes it may be of your health or relationship with your family.....

That goal will be your "Main goal". You have to take it as a central purpose of your success and the starting point of your journey.

This goal should be your 'mission' and central point to all your programmes.

Some Principles to Set Goals

To set your goals and fulfil those goals, you have to follow some principles:

- **First – Link between the goals**

  There should be a link between your goals to prevent the inconsistency or conflict.

  For example, your goal is to achieve successful business or earn profits at the same time you should not feel like spending half day with your children or friends, because there is no consistency between these two goals.

  Your goals should be supportive to one another and strengthening, but should not clash with one another.

- **Second – Taking goals as challenges**

  Your goals should make you rigid on one hand and liberal on the other hand.

  To fulfill your goals you need 50% opportunities so that you can move forward to achieve them. Suppose if you look at only 20% opportunities helpless and sad.

  So chose the goals that have 50% opportunities in the initial stage itself. Later you can take up the goals that have 40% or 30% or 20% opportunities and achieve them with excitement.

- **Third -Qualitative**

  As the goals you set physically should be clear and concrete, so also in the same level they have to resemble your inner life and relationships.

  For example, if one of your goals is to build a beautiful mansion for your family to live in and after achieving the first goal, your second goal should be qualitative like spending time happily and patiently with them. These two goals will connect to one another and serve as a link between your inner life and outer life.

- **Fourth – Short-term Goals and Long-term Goals**

  For every person there are some goals which can be fulfilled in 5 years, 10 years, 20 years.. These are called as short-term goal and long term goals.

Either in business or your career or personal planning one should achieve his short-term goals within a period of 90 days.

Long-term goals can be achieved within two or three years of duration.

During this period, one should move forward with continuous motivation.

Recognising the Goals

In order to know what type of goals you want to set in your life try to answer the following questions repeatedly. For this, take one white paper, write down the following questions and answer them:

- First question – what are the five important values?
- Second question –what are the three important goals right now?
- Third question –if you are aware that you live only for six months, how do you live those six months?
- Fourth question – suppose if you receive fifty lakhs tax free amount as a lottery prize, how do spend you that money?
- Fifth question – what is the thing that you always wanted to do but unable to do because of fear?
- Sixth question – which type of work gives you the most pleasure in your life? Which aspect in you will help to improve your self-esteem?
- Seventh question – If God appears in front of you and asks you to choose a desire so that he will fulfill it for you, which one you wish for?

After answering all the above-mentioned questions read all the answers and think again. From those answers pick up one of the most important aspect of your life and get ready to achieve it.....

Twelve-fold Programme

This twelve-fold programme will help you to fulfil your desire. This programme may appear to be simple but it gives wonderful results to fulfill your goals. It gives you clarity to reach your destination.

- **First**

  To Develop a Burning Desire – In order to fulfill any task one should always need a burning desire. This burning desire gives us the motivation to achieve the things that we wish.

- **Second**

  To Strengthen Your Confidence – To achieve the goal first you have to activate your subconscious mind. To activate it, you should have a strong belief that you can fulfil the goal. Only through 'confidence', your psychological powers are activated. Those goals also should be near to the reality. Suppose you want to earn money. Your goal should not be earning huge income in a year. Instead, plan to increase your income yearly to 10% or 20% or 30%. So set the goals that are possible and move forward with confidence and positive attitude. Success will be yours.

- **Third**

  Write on a Paper – It is good to write your aspirations and goals of your life on a piece of paper. Unless you write them on the paper, remain like desires and fantasies. Many people with lack of confidence never like to write their goals on the paper. They doubt whether those goals will fulfil or not. But the fact is that when you write down your goals on the paper immediately your sub-conscious mind keeps aside your 'fear of failure' and motivates you to fulfil your goals.

- **Fourth**

  Write down the list of profits you gain by achieving the goal – By writing down the profits, they will act as driving force and motivation and leads you forward. The profits you write as a list will become the reasons for your goals. The more you look at the reasons (profits) the more you are motivated to fulfil your goals.

Reasons That Lead You Forward

So also achieving the goals! Once a young man came to Socrates and said, "I want to learn everything you know. I want your wisdom".

To that Socrates responded, "Follow me to that river."

"Take a close look and tell me what you see."

The young man replied, "I see only the river of course."

Socrates told him to peep down into the water and asked him to look closer.

As he peered over bank and leaned closer, Socrates grabbed the man's head and shoved it under water!!!

The man tried to escape and flailed his arms wildly as he was getting choked.

But Socrates' strong grip kept his head submerged in water just a little more time!

As the young man continued to struggle, finally Socrates released his grip and let his head come out of water.

"Are you crazy old man? You want to kill me?" shouted the young man gasping for his breath.

Socrates asked him, "When I was holding your head under water, what is that first thing you needed most? What did you want more than anything else?"

"I wanted to breathe I wanted air of course", said the man still panting.

So Socrates said, "If and when you want wisdom that badly like you wanted air, then you come to me!"

When you look at the profits, satisfaction and gifts gained by achieving the goals, this will lit fire in your mind to achieve the goals you set.

So definitely you have to write the list of profits!

- ❑ **Fifth**

  Assess your Present Condition – Suppose your goal is to reduce your weight. First, learn about your present weight. Examine how much you have put up over weight.

  So also, you want to earn a sum of amount. First know your bank balance, property, and then figure out how to earn the remaining amount.

  This type of assessment will help you to measure your progress. The logic in it is:-

  If you know clearly from where you are starting and how far you are going, definitely you'll reach that point

- ❑ **Sixth**

  Set a Deadline - "There are impossible deadlines but there are no impossible goals."

  To fulfil some goals it is very important to set deadline at the same time it is also impossible to set deadline for some goals.

  You can set deadline to some of the aspects like earning money, reducing the body weight etc...

  But you can't set deadline for personal matters like to increase patience, self-discipline, molding the character etc...

  Some people will not set deadline to any aspect with a fear that they may fail to achieve the goals.

People should be optimistic regarding this aspect. Suppose if they fail to complete it within a specific time they can prolong it and set another date.

When you are capable of achieving your goals, when your planning is comprehensive and if you put your total efforts to fulfil the planning, in 80% cases, definitely you will achieve the goals....

- **Seventh**

Write down the list of obstacles that are standing between you and your goal - It is natural to come across great obstacles to achieve bi success. If there are no obstacles, the goal you chose will be seen normal! After writing all the obstacles as a list try to find out the main 'obstacle'!That obstacle may arise due to internal force or external force.During such situations question yourself-"To achieve the goal do I need to change myself?"

Or

"To achieve the goal do I need to improve my capabilities and educational talents?"

The external factors that stand as barriers between you and your goals are may be your job or any wrong relationship.

In such conditions, again you have to start your goals from the beginning. Now you question yourself the second question-

"What are my limitations?".

This limiting step is called as Bottleneck.

If you overcome this Bottleneck, you can come close to your goals.

- **Eighth**

To know additional information to achieve your goal - It is your duty to collect complete information to achieve your gl!

Write down the information, talents, skills and capabilities of it as a list. Now try to learn those aspects.

It may be through studying the books, by consulting the specialists, by taking the advices etc.

So it is very important to collect information and knowledge through any means!!

- **Ninth**

Write down the names of the persons who help you to reach your goals - This list may contain the names of your family members, your boss, your customers, your bankers, your business partners, your friends.......

Now write down the names of persons as a list according to the prominence.While taking help from them ask the following question to yourself- "Can I help him in turn for his help?"

Watch many successful people in the society before taking help from others they will help others and gain lot of goodwill. Later they will use this goodwill as an investment.

To gain qualitative and quantitative help from others first they should render a lot of service to them.

- **Tenth**

Planning - Four things are important for the planning. They are paper, pen, your goal and you. After setting it, now write comprehensively on a paper.

  - What are you wishing for?
  - In 'how much' time you want to have it?
  - Why are you wishing for it?
  - 'Where' do you want to start your efforts to achieve it?
  - What 'information' you have to overcome?
  - Whose 'help' you need?

  If write the answers for the above-mentioned questions, then are ready with your complete master plan.

  You can alter the plans! Once when you are with the master plan, get ready to put your efforts.

  But remember one thing!

  Nobody can't prepare perfect planning so try to accept that there may be some defects in it and get ready for it...

- **Eleventh**

Visualising the result/results – Visualise the results and the conditions once when you achieve your goals or ambitions. It's also called as 'daydream'.

But you shouldn't addict to this daydream. Only in some situations, you have to use this visualisation to give a 'kick' and make you move forward to reach your goal.

By visualisation, your sub-conscious mind activates and the all your psychological powers are centred around your goals. This will enhance your will-power.

- ❑ **Twelfth**

  Taking firm decisions that you are not going to stop in the middle under any circumstances – You should not turn away from your goal under any circumstances. Even you shouldn't let that idea enter into your mind.

  As long as you move forward to reach your goal without stopping in the middle, it will take you nearer and nearer towards your destination.

Success, Making It a Habit

Once after setting your goals and plans, you have to decide not to stop your efforts in the middle under any circumstances, until you achieve your goals.

Through continuous efforts and by keeping pace with the programmes, defining your goals according to the programmes comes under imposing self-discipline and success habits.

This makes you to put some daily endeavour to your goals and leads you towards your achievements. This is what success habit means! "Nothing succeeds like success."

Developing "success habit" is a trait of the wise!

Daily in the morning, evening and during the night time, before you go to sleep, you must analyse and think about it always.

Daily, you have to examine yourself what are your contributions that day in order to receive success.

Like this, your dreams of success and happiness will come true!

Start with the goal setting, shape up into a planning with your creativity and positive thoughts. Maintain the pace through your will-power and self-discipline which will lead you towards the goals that you are going to achieve…

As a result, you can become the 'winner' in the end.

"BE WHAT YOU WANT TO BE."

Motivation

The driving force that makes us to do any task is known as *motivation.* Suppose you are reading this book, "Success Management".

You are so involved in reading this book that except this book, you are not interested in reading any other book or doing anyother task. The reason behind this type of reading is motivation.

You need the following to achieve success in life and earn more money, fame, etc.

You are reading this book with a hope to seek answers to the above-mentioned aspects and many other aspects of life, to better your present conditions as well as your future. Isn't it??

That driving force which is working in you right now is motivation!

So to do anything at any time is only because of motivation.

It is very surprising to learn but even sitting in an easy chair and lazily spending time takes place only because of motivation.

Like this....

Without motivation we can't do anything.

Whatever task we carry out, it is either big or small happens only because of motivation.

Motivation-Motive

The definition for Motive is an idea, belief, or emotion that impels a person to act in accordance with that state of mind.

Any person will not to do anything without any motive in his mind.

Motivation encourages us to do actions.

Previously, there was an opinion that through gifts, rallies, competitions and provoking lectures, men can be motivated and work can be extracted from them. But the modern psychologists oppose that opinion and they say that-

Gifts, money, lectures, rallies and competitions are the incentives or inspirations that push a man into action, but not the motivation.

Motivation is a condition that comes from within a person.

Motivation is an emotional state-

Everyone has to be motivated within him or her because external factors like any person or any power can't motivate anybody!

Anytime, you should do "what you want to do" but never do," what you don't like to do."

Things you want to do is motivation!

Physical and psychological aspects that motivate us in our lives are as follows:

- ❑ Anticipation towards life
- ❑ Hunger
- ❑ Thirst
- ❑ Love
- ❑ Vengeance, etc…

If the emotion combines with the above-mentioned aspects, motivation becomes stronger.

Two main emotions that influence the motivation in man- desire, fear.

Both the emotions are repellant show the equivalent results.

Desire yields positive motivation and fear yields negative motivation.

Negative emotion that comes out of fear is very powerful.

Fear will not let us do anything. It destroys our plans that are made to achieve our goals and finally pushes us into failures.

But the positive emotion that comes out of desire is like a strong magnet which pushes us towards our goals. It makes us victorious by fulfilling the plans constructively.

Desires, Fear- both are different poles- these two poles push us into opposite directions.

'Fear' makes us to look back into the past

'Desire' makes us to look at the future

'Fear' reminds us of our past failures, distress, grief and unhappiness, makes us depressed and doesn't allow us to do anything.

'desire' reminds us of our victories and pleasures- It replays them- make us feel that once again they happen in our life.

A person who suffers from fear thinks:

"I can't do this work"

"Taking up this work means taking up the risk"

"How good if it happens like this..."

A person who has a burning desire and optimistic attitude feels:

"I want that"

"I'll do this work"

"I can do this work"

"I see many opportunities in it".

Desire and fear both will create tension in a person.

Desire is an emotional situation that is between "where you are today" and "where you are going to reach"!

"Desire' creates positive tension in man

"Fear" creates negative tension in man.

Fear causes mental stress, anxiety, different types of ailments and enmity towards others.

Extreme fear takes the man towards the death.

But the positive tension which arises because of desire works like an arrow aimed at the goal.

Positive tension gives a thrill like feeling.

Always we move forward according to our thoughts. The thoughts are related to our desire we step towards our goals.

But if the thoughts are related to our fear we step towards the opposite direction of our goals.

So always it is good think according to your desires!

Never Think of the Problems but Think about the Solutions

They take risks as opportunities to achieve success. They foresee the rewards and profits. They will not fear for the penalties of the failures.

Success can't be achieved through potentialities, talents, wisdom, IQ, comforts and conveniences or by birth.

Even after having all the above said aspects, if he doesn't have zeal, then it is futile.

Only when a person has this zeal then he can achieve success.

That zeal is motivation- motivation arising from the 'desire'!

So if you have the 'desire', then you will try to put all your efforts to gather your capabilities!

'Desire' Arouses the Zeal to Win in a Man

When the 'zeal to win' is driving him forward, there is no cause or time to be defeated……

Decision Making

"It is your moments of decision that your destiny is shaped"

— Anthony Robbins

How will be your life after ten years?

Are you able to be better position or worse than before? Or you are going to stay in the same condition without any progress?

Can you answer these questions??

Your answer for the question is- how will be the life after ten years depends upon the 'decision you take today' or 'not taking any decision'!

The decisions we take will lead to various activities and various activities gives various results.

So

What results we are getting today and in what shape our life is- everything depends upon the decision we made in the past.

If you have taken another decision, today your life will be different. Not only your life even your family members life too.

Once you think,

Examine your ten years of your life or twenty years of your life (according to your age). If you have taken another decision regarding the important aspect of your life, today can you lead this kind of life?

Suppose- imagine that you are a doctor. In your college days, instead of medicine, if you had opted for engineering or science or commerce, today what would have been your life? Are you satisfied with your life? Are you living it qualitatively?

Regarding your life partner, if you have selected another person as your spouse your children look with different features, there will be a slight difference in the aspects of comforts, conveniences and peace of mind.

The decisions we take in our life change our destiny.

The reason, today you are able to enjoy

Success in all aspects is-

only because of your past efforts

and the price you paid.

Beliefs

While taking decisions, the beliefs in us will also play an important role. Because of these beliefs, many times without questioning 'what is this' and without any thought, we take decisions based on our beliefs.

Personal beliefs are fixed in our childhood. We depend upon our parents for every decision because at that stage we don't have the capability to analyse the incident or experience to think about the good or bad.

During that tender age when you do mistake knowingly or knowingly and when the parents always pass the comments by saying, "you are fit for nothing" or "you can't do anything", that comments are strongly imprinted in the mind.

This feeling is so strongly fixed in the mind that even in the future you are afraid to take decisions by thinking that you are inferior and believe that your decisions will lead to failure.

It is all because of your belief, which fixed in your mind that you are inferior. These types of persons hesitate to take the responsibility of their life. They can't achieve success.

Goals are Important

If you have clear-cut goals in the aspects of where you are now and where do you want to go in your life, then it will be easier for you to take decisions.

In day-to-day life, we have to take many decisions regarding, to leave the job or not, to ask a hike in the income or not, to go this way or that way, to start the business with that person or not, etc...

When you are well aware of your chief ambition, main aspiration and long-term goals of your lifes it will be easier to take decisions.....

For example, your goal is to become a computer engineer. So, you will take all the educational decisions that will lead you towards your goal.

So it is important to have a goal in your life. By setting goals, your life will be come meaningful, and it also gives a value to your life.

Facing the problems always is
Life!!
The secret of victory lies in
how you react towards that
Problem!!

According to the Values

Take decisions according to the values you set for in your lives.

If you give value to friendship, turn off the T.V and try to meet people, develop acquaintances, etc. By doing so, you can develop friendship with many people.

Similarly give equal importance to values like education, career, self-improvement, health, wealth, etc.

Precautions While Taking Decisions

- **Specifically you have to define your goal**: your goal should be specific.
  - For example, you shouldn't think vaguely "I have to gain computer knowledge". You should be clear like, I have to learn MS office in computers or Excel or JAVA etc....
  - So also, instead of thinking, "I have to earn more Money", you have to think, "By the time, I reach this age, I have to earn this much of amount".
- **Research**: Before taking a decision, you have to know the primary information and the secondary information regarding a particular aspect.
  - Suppose if you want to buy a personal computer, speak with three or four sales representatives. Not only try to learn the good things of that company but also ask the defects of the other company models.
  - By doing this, you will be able to know the various companies and computer models as well as their plus and minus points.
  - Then meet the people who have already bought and are using the same company computer that you want to buy. Ask them whether there are any practical defects. So also

collect as much information as possible from computer journals. This is all secondary information.

- Combine these two sources and now you take decision to buy the computer according to your need.
- You can follow the same pattern regarding to do higher studies or business

- **Think about the Risks**: some people think about the results of their decisions and never take any decisions with the fear of risk. They want to skip the decision-making.
  - When you have the fear of the risk question yourself the following question:
  - "Suppose If I take this decision and when it fails, what do I lose?"
  - If that decision gives a great loss, try to avoid that decision.
  - Research about it and search for other decisions.
  - Even if you face failure with the decision you take but you will learn some lesson from it. But the failure should cause less damage for you.
  - Surprising fact is that sometimes you will be closer to success with your faults. The people who achieved wonderful success are normal human beings and committed many mistakes.
- **Analysis**: Sometimes you will be in hesitation whether to do or not to do, at that time you lose your analysis power.
  - When you are disturbed with the problems, stop thinking about it and get relaxed. Later take a paper and pen and sit aside.
  - Write down on the paper the decision you get in your mind and the reasons for taking that decision or the reasons for not taking that decision.
  - Now analyse the pros and cons of it and take the useful decision.
  - For example, you want to buy new vehicle to go to office regularly on time. The vehicle may be a car. Now analyse it in the following manner.

If the reason you say is very important give 10 marks, if there is no importance at all give 1mark. In this manner according to the prominence, grade between 1 and 10-

Look at the following box-

Goal : Daily going to the office on time **Decision : To buy a new car**			
Reasons to Buy	**Marks**	**Reasons not to Buy**	**Marks**
Because of the new car, there won't be any repairs and can go to office on time.	8	Old car is running good.	8
I'll feel 'better' in the new car.	7	In four or five months later new models are arriving in the market so I'll wait till then and buy latest model.	8
My image increases if I buy a new car.	5	My economic condition is not good	10
Total	20	Total	26
Result: Not to buy a new car The things that have to be done: To spend some money and repair the car To give a better image when ever relatives and clients visit home to take a rented deluxe car.			

- Do any one Definitely: Always military officers are given an advice. When they are in danger, they should not be still. They have to involve in any action even if there is no use.
  - In other words, even in disastrous conditions they have to do something but should not be motionless.
  - Even if you don't want to take any decision, you have to set a time limit and take a decision.
  - If you are in a dark room without any action, you'll be in the darkness. If you somehow or other manage try to walk in it you'll find the wall and if you walk beside the wall then you'll reach the door or window or light switch.
  - So also with the decision making.....

Niagara Syndrome

Many of us do not take conscious decisions, but take momentary decisions according to the context and need. Sometimes, we take decisions according to the advices of others.

This type of attitude is called as "Niagara Syndrome".

- ❑ Life is like a gently flowing river journey. Many people begin this journey without having a clear idea of where they want to end up and simply go with the flow, eventually getting caught-up in the currents as a result, they feel out of control and they merely go with the flow. They remain in this unconscious state until one day the sound of the raging water awakens them and they discover that they are five feet from Niagara Falls in a boat with no oars. At this point, they take the fall.
- ❑ Sometimes it's an emotional fall, sometimes it's physical fall, sometimes it's a financial fall....
- ❑ It's likely that whatever challenges you have in your life currently could have been avoided by some better decisions upstream.

It Should Give Long-term Results

The decisions we should yield long-term results than short-term results or comforts. So now only we have to decide how we are going to live or what we want to be after five years or ten years. Accordingly, we have to note down constructive planning.

Keep the following aspects in your mind while you take those types of decisions. They are:

- ❑ No one can achieve success in one single night itself.
- ❑ You should be ready with long-term planning and try hard to put into action.
- ❑ In the way of your journey towards the success each moment, you have to use every opportunity and prospect your life gives.
- ❑ In the decisions you take there are no failures- just 'results'. Sometimes you won't get the result you wish but it's not the failure. Through this experience you can get the chance to take better decision.
- ❑ The decisions you take will not yield immediate results but once when you stick to them they can yield long-term results.

- ❑ To achieve success first we should inculcate self-discipline and look at the long-term results. Never satisfy with temporary results and benefits-

  While taking decisions

  - ➤ First, you have to decide what you want
  - ➤ Make proper planning to achieve it
  - ➤ Take up the necessary progression
  - ➤ Until you achieve the result move forward by making necessary changes whenever the situation demands.....

    Another aspect

    Are you now reading this book to achieve success in any aspect related to you. Isn't it??

    If you can't put these principles in practice it is a mere waste of reading this book.

    So read this book with an intention to practice these principles which will be a benefit in your life. Then only you can achieve success.....

"If you have more enemies than friends, it's time to examine your mental attitude." — **Napoleon Hill**

Success Formula-3

You have to set a high goal that is necessary to your life and always think about it in your mind. Consider it as a major goal.

- ❑ Set some sub-goals in order to achieve the major goal. Those goals should not clash with major goal. These sub-goals, some have to be achieved immediately, some during a period of time and some have to be achieved in the long run of time.
- ❑ Your desire, whatever you are wishing for should always penetrate in your mind and that desire should be very clear.
- ❑ Assess the things that you have to lose to achieve your goals and be prepared to lose them.
- ❑ Decide the date to fulfill your wish.
- ❑ Prepare a planning to fulfill your wish and immediately implement that planning.

- The planning you prepare to achieve your wish should be very clear. Write it in detail on a paper.
- Write down clearly about your wish, the time limit to achieve it, what things you are losing to fulfill your wish etc...
- Every day morning and evening read it and feel it. You should also feel the emotion how it would be like after achieving it.
- Always self-examine yourself whether you are going in a correct direction or not. This will ensure you to go in the correct or the right direction.

  To achieve cent percent success, regularly read books, think, and practise time management. Always have a positive attitude towards your family and yourself. Take care to concentrate on your goals and never divert from them.

Self-Destruction Qualities

Some people in the world are always achieve success in any given task. Some other people always face failure. What is the reason for this? When we look at the second type of persons we feel that 'they are unlucky' isn't it??

Is there any misfortune?? Is it responsible for some persons failure??

When your scooter or car doesn't work properly, you will take it to a mechanic. He will test it and repair it.

So also if you are sick the doctor according to the symptoms prescribes medicines.

But when you face a problem in your life nobody will come to your rescue. You have to find out the reasons and set right them.

In many situations we are responsible for our failures. let's examine these reasons of failure or self-destruction qualities :

Qualities of Self-Destruction

Throwing the blame on others

It is not that we are worrying about what people will think of us. But blaming others for all our miseries, problems and failures!

The human quality of blaming others is from primitive days. In olden days when a person becomes sick people use to throw that blame on witch or wizard. Still in the 21st century, we can see these types of beliefs in some under developed countries and villages.

Ancient man thought, "The sickness came because of black magic" and modern medicine thinks, "It's because of some reason."

So also primitive man thought fortune and misfortune are the reasons for his success or failures. Modern man's educated and more sophisticated brain thinks differently "what are the reasons for this failure? What defect in me brought this failure?? What factors are responsible for this failure??".

Here are some examples how the people throw blame on others:

- A small child says that his brother or sister is responsible for his mistake.
- A school child throws blame on his teacher for not getting marks in the exams
- A scooterist says that the fellow who comes in the opposite direction is responsible for the accident.
- A husband who quarrels with his wife says that she is always quarrelsome.

You have to come out of this habit of throwing blame on others and set right your defects.

Self-blame

Second bad quality that throws a person into failures is self-blame.

- "All this happened only because of me"
- "I am a useless person, that's why it happened like this!"
- "Always it happens to me like this, I have a defect in me"

These are the thoughts that a person gets whenever he face a failure. These types of self-blaming thoughts are dangerous. These thoughts give rise to inferiority feeling and insecurity feeling. He can't move forward in his life. These thoughts of self-blame are like 'weeds' in the garden of mind.

These types of persons search their happiness in the failures. They face failure in every attempt they make.

Self-blame is more dangerous than self-pity. Because self-blame is the reason for self-pity.

Self-blame means to hold responsible or to find fault with them. Through this, a person brings self-destruction. Extreme self-blame leads to guilty feeling. It also closes the doors of self-development. Later it makes a person to suffer from melancholia.

That's why whenever a person faces failures he has to search for the reasons but never try to blame himself.

- **Without any goals**: No person in this world is without any goal. Every person has one or other goal.

- To obtain a degree, to get a job, to nurture the children, to earn 'some particular amount of' wealth etc.. like this every one has big or small goal.
- But the goal he chooses should be a useful one. There is a story related to this. One day a dog made a bet with other dogs saying "of all the animals that walk on four legs, I will run faster than those animals." Then they spotted a rabbit going that way. The other dogs asked this dog to catch that rabbit. So the dog chased the rabbit. The rabbit darted this way and that way around trees and open field. Finally it escaped into bushes. Looking at this the other dogs made fun of it. For that the tired dog replied like this- "Remember rabbit is running for its life. It is its goal and I am chasing it for fun without any goal. That's why it has won and I lost".

Yes it's true!

Our goals should be serious and useful to our life. If there is no seriousness, even the talents are wasted and we can't achieve any success.

- **Setting wrong goals:** A young man who lived in Beijing, china use to see gold daily in his dream. One day immediately after raising up from bed he put on the new clothes and went to market. Straight away went to a gold shop and collected whatever gold he saw in into his bag and left that place. The police arrested him and questioned him "how dare to do it in front of all?" for that he answered, "I didn't see there anybody except gold".

This is blind goal! Whether it is regarding gold or fame or power your goal should not be blind. Your goal shouldn't bring any loss to others or take away happiness from you. It shouldn't kill your conscience.

A person wants to earn crores of money or wants to become a big officer. For that he strives hard. He foregoes his happiness, comforts and moves forward. Finally he succeeds.

But by the time, he achieves all things he will be in his sixties or seventies. What can he enjoy at this stage? Or if he dies suddenly after achieving all these things, all his efforts and achievements go waste. This type of goal is a wrong goal!

Instead, he has to set a goal that has to be fulfilled at the age of 40 or 45. **The goals a person wants o fulfill shouldn't take away**

his happiness or comforts. The attempts to achieve the goals should give him pleasure but not regrets or repentance.

- **Wanted to go for short-cut methods**: Many of us unknowingly want to reach the destination in a shortest route. It is called as 'short cut methods'. This is an instinctive desire. In order to achieve the success many of them search for these short cuts. For example:
  - Instead of working hard, a person wants to reach higher position in his career simply by impressing his higher officials. This type of attitude makes the officers feel happy but inside they look down at the person.
  - So also a person who want to earn huge amount will think to get that amount overnight without any effort. To achieve it he is ready to deceive the law, deceive his own friends, leave the moral values and lead deceitful life.

All these aspects at first appear to give temporary results but in the end bring many problems. For example, those problems are in the following manner:

- It brings a bad remark on his character. Even if the people praise in front of him but talk low of him on his back.
- Family relations are spoiled. There will be artificiality in the family life.
- Health spoils. The thoughts to reach higher position cause mental stress and this stress will lead to high B.P, Heart attacks, ulcers in the stomach and other types of sickness.
- The curiosity to reach higher position makes a man to leave the established rules in the society like honesty, truthfulness and decency. These aspects make him to lose self-respect and causes unhappiness....

  So .....

  Instead of choosing short-cut methods, if he goes in a correct method with hard work and in a legal way, he can improve self-respect, and also extract respect from the society.

- **Not taking care of minute matters:** Many persons to achieve their goals always concern about the big persons who are far away or big matters which are far behind, but don't care about the small persons who are very near or small matters which are near to them. It is very surprising aspect!

In this world, no person is small, no job is small or nothing is small. The persons may be different or the jobs may be different. It may be easier to handle them or the result may be small. **But don't forget that the small jobs, small people act like the foundation stones for your success. Your greatness lies in identifying those small things.**

If you can't handle the small aspects or small people, sometimes these small aspects stand as obstacles for your success.

A surgeon will not neglect any device by saying it is useless. Each device has its own importance. While operating a patient he will not neglect any small aspect, because it is life and death situation for the patient. So also a qualified lawyer will not miss any small legal point as this point is very crucial to his client.

- **To quit in the middle**: In 1942, an incident had taken place in Venezuela, three persons are searching for diamonds in the pebbles of Venezuelan riverbed. They were exhausted mentally, physically and emotionally. Their clothes were tattered and their spirits weak. A person called Rafael Solano, who was physically exhausted and defeated, announced to his companions-

  "I'm through. There's no use going on any longer. See this pebble. It makes 999,999, I've picked up without finding one diamond. One more pebble makes a million, but what's the use? I quit!"

  "Pick up one more and make it a million," one man said. Solano consented and pulled forth a stone the size of a hen's egg. It was different from the others, and the crew soon realized they had a diamond. It is reported that Harry Winston, a New York jewel dealer, paid Rafael Solano $200,000 for that millionth pebble. The stone was named the Liberator and to date, it is the largest and purest diamond ever found."

  If Rafael Solano gave up and did not pick a pebble one more time, he would not have discovered the largest and purest diamond named Liberator. The millionth pebble made him famous and rich. So the main reason for the failure is to give up in the middle of a work.

  The difference that lies between success and failure is not the wrong 'start' but only the wrong 'stop'.

  It is foolish to stop in the middle of the any given task. You need a strong determination to move forward in any difficult situation.

Moving forward without giving up in the middle itself is defeating the failure! Man's ability is known only when he sets his mind to defeat the failure!!

- **Unable to understand the victory**: Success is a like an inconsistent goddess it will throw us in many difficult situations when we are trying to bring it under our control.

  The great emperor Napoleon says-

  "The most dangerous moment comes with the victory!!"

  Yes, it's true because success brings overconfidence in a person. When a small problem arises he gets irritated and feels that even after achieving success, why to face problems? Actually, he is unable to understand the success.

  There is no end to success. It's a continuous process. When you stop in the middle with few achievements success becomes mere waste. An intellectual says-

  "Instead of sitting on the edge of the sword, man can do anything with it". So also it is with success!

  Here we can take the example of Dr. N.T.Rama Rao, a famous erstwhile actor and former chief minister of Andhra Pradesh, India. His struggle for power was comfortably achieved. But after getting the power, he was unable to protect it, because he felt it was enough and kept it in the hands of his people whom he believed in.

  Instead of it, if he had understood the fact that he has to continue his struggle alone on his own, he might have reached a higher position in Indian politics. So he defeated failure, but was unable to defeat victory. It was his weakness....

- **To exhibit the authority:** To any person, after achieving success there arises a need to exhibit his power. Your authority itself reveals that you are nearer to success.

  Here are some techniques and principles to exhibit your authority:

  - Your instructions should be simple and brief. Your subordinates should execute them without raising any questions.
  - If there response is not acceptable to you, strictly respond and instruct them to follow your orders.
  - Never try to share your personal matters and personal life with your subordinates.

- When a work is done according to your instructions, you have to accept the victory in a decent manner as if you are aware of it.
- While giving a task and speaking with your subordinates, never look straight into their eyes but look at their forehead above the eyebrows. They should feel that your words are very important.
- Never try to develop friendship with them or encourage such efforts from them. Even if you have made a mistake don't accept it before them. Never say, "I made an error" or "I made a mistake", instead of that say, "I would have achieved success if I would have solved this problem... in some another manner."

Failures Teach Lessons

A young fellow attends many interviews but never secures any job. Another young fellow moves around a beautiful girl who resembles Madhuri Dixit but can't gain her love. An employee works sincerely in his office but can't get the favour of his higher officials.

In the same manner some people whatever task they choose they face hurdles. They can't achieve any task successfully.

These are all the symptoms of failure!

In any failure, there will be 30% adverse conditions and 70% defects of that person. In some situations failures occur cent percent because of the defects of a person.

These defects are like lack of self-confidence, lack of determination and effort, to depress quickly, pessimistic attitude, unable to set a goal etc..! In many situations these defects in man are the reasons for failure.

Here are some examples to comfort the persons who are in confusion with continuous failures. These examples also throw out the depression in these kinds of persons.

National Joke Turned to National Pride

In Australia there is a Danish architect called Jorn Utzon. He got 5 million dollar contract to construct an auditorium. He started the construction soon after receiving the order. Months and years passed but there is no progress. Mean while expenses are growing more and more. People thought that there is a mistake in his design. He was unable to succeed even after changing his plan. Budget has gone high. Instead of 5 million, it reached 25 million, 50 million and finally 75 millions. Still the construction hasn't completed. The press criticized him. The whole project has become a national joke. At last, it was completed in 10 years with an expense of 100 million dollars.

What will you do when you are in the place of that Architect?

You will become depressed and disappointed all through your life. Isn't it??

But Jorn didn't feel at all. He was deeply immersed in the construction work with lot of determination and effort. When the construction was finished people looked at it and marveled at its beauty.

Out of all the constructions of the 20th century, it has become the wonderful construction. The people of Australia considered it as one of the wonders of their country. Every year Australia is getting millions of dollars from the visitors who come to visit this construction.

Do you know the name of that famous construction?

It's Sydney Opera House!

If the architect has stopped in the middle of the construction with disappointment because of the increasing expenses, Will it be completed? Will it get a great name?!

Lincoln's Failures

Do you believe that the greatest personality and outstanding leader Abraham Lincoln has lost seven times in the elections??

Failures of the Creator of Superman

We are all aware of the superman comic. At first, every comic publisher rejected the script of the superman saying that it is not good. After many efforts, the publishers of detective comics accepted to publish it. And it got a bumper success. Each book was sold into million copies.

Do you know the creator of that comic- superman?

They are two school going young boys!!

The Successful Writer

Mary Higgins Clark is an American author of suspense novels. Her husband died leaving the young widow to care for five children. She has no university education. She worked as a secretary and flight attendant to support the family. But the income is not sufficient to run the family. Clark decided to try her hand at books. When she wrote her first book, it has been rejected forty times before a magazine in Chicago bought it for one hundred dollars.

Over the next few decades, the prolific Clark wrote more than two dozen suspense novels that sold over 80 million copies in the United States alone. She is the bestselling fiction author in France and has held numerous posts among mystery genre circles, including president of Mystery Writers of America and Chairman of the International Crime Congress. She is also the inspiration for the Mystery Writers of America's Mary Higgins Clark Award. In addition to writing, she returned to school to earn her philosophy degree from Fordham University.

Where are the children? A Cry in the Night, The Cradle will Fall, Weep No More, My Lady, etc are some of the best sellers written by her....

Problems of the Beasts

Of all the beasts of Asian Continent, Bengal Royal Tiger is the most dangerous one. When it tries to hunt 10 times only once it catches its prey. Even African Lion when it tries 10 times to catch its prey it succeeds only once.

These are some of the examples to show how to face the failures.

So...

Whenever you face any failure, don't get depressed. It's not the quality of the wise. The person who blame himself for the failure and who possess self-pity will not grow up in his life.

Some principles to the people who possess self-pity:

- In problems, never lose courage and confidence.
- Don't look at failures and assume them as big.
- Never imagine negative aspects.
- Face the failures silently with a strong mind.
- Without letting, any negative feelings into the mind compete with the failures boldly.

These are the qualities of successful persons.

To Exhibit Authority

In order to get the things done in a proper manner, one has to show less authority as far as possible on the subordinates. Excessive authority gives a bad picture of you. Some subordinates who have individuality will rebel against you.

- Remember – you have to exhibit your authority only to fulfill your goal or to make your subordinates follow your instructions.
- When they are following your orders promptly, then there is no need of constant reminding that you are their boss.

- There is a rule in the military that the officers should not socialize with the soldier. If he knows the weakness of his officer, sometimes he will deny obeying the commands of his officer. Same rule is applicable here.
- If an official has any doubts he should clarify those doubts through other or from other source but shouldn't ask his subordinates.
- Remember - exhibiting authority is only to achieve success but not to humiliate the subordinates!
- In front of the subordinates, an officer should act like a teacher before the students, like a father before the children. Same feeling has to be created in their minds and never behave like a tyrant or let that feeling in them.......

How to Earn Money?

We are aware that in these modern days, money is given a lot of importance than any other thing! Because of money, many times in our life, our emotions are disturbed. Many persons for the sake of money neglect many important and valuable aspects of their life.

To earn money, they are not even ready to spend their time with their family, friends and sometimes neglect their health to earn money.

There is an inseparable relation between money and sorrow, suffering, pain and grief.

For some people money is a mystery. For some people it is like a sour grapes. For some people it causes pride, for some it causes envy and some people reject it.

What is truth in it? What is the reality?

When we look at it intellectually, money is used to exchange things. Money will simplify the process of sharing, changing and creating.

Lack of money creates a feeling of insecurity, anxiety, depression, worry, anger etc.... in a person makes him lose his confidence.

Have you seen any person, corporation, or company that hasn't undergone economical stress?

Many of them think that if they have sufficient money, they can clear their problems but it's not correct in that process they will struck up without liberty.

It is also ridicule if you say that a person after earning money, liberated from economical stress can't inculcate values in others.

If you observe for two days at Banjara Hills and Jubilee Hills in Hyderabad, the buildings, vehicles and the people, you are astonished and feel that how these people has acquired unbelievable wealth and maintaining them. Also, feel that in your lifetime you can't reach to that position.

Even after having a strong desire to earn money, still you are unable to acquire wealth, the reason might be a strong defect in economical foundation. The defects can be in various forms:

In the form of your moral values, in the form of two contradictory values, in the form of beliefs, proper planning, lack of determination, etc. All these lead to financial failures.

Misconceptions

Many of us have misconceptions upon the people who around us reach to a higher status from lower status by earning the money.

- That they have earned the money in a wrong way, by deceiving the innocent people, committed many illegal things etc... like this people will think about them.

These types of feelings are regarding others. Even about ourselves, we have some negative feelings regarding the earning of the money. They are:

- To earn huge amount we have to work hard day and night without any rest. By the time, we earn that income we will become tired, old and in this situation we can't enjoy that earnings, so earning money is nothing but greediness...
- In the process of earning money we may lose, our moral values and religious belief. So it is better to be content with what we have.

In reality, these are all partial facts. But in some situations and in somebody's life it's not correct.

If you really have the zeal to earn money and become rich, without forgoing the moral values or your complete youth you can become rich.

But to achieve it you need proper planning and a strong determination to implement that planning. As said in this book, you should possess self-confidence, self-esteem, self-discipline, mental stability, will-power and optimism in equal ratios.

First, you should take away the above said misconceptions on money from your mind. Because:

If you think that money is bad, and huge amounts are acquired only by wrong means, also if you believe that because of money you have to lose your values, comforts etc., then these thoughts will reach your subconscious mind and they will send wrong signals to your brain.

Because of these wrong signals, you can't get motivation to become rich. You will be in the same condition without any furthes improvements.

Economic Chemistry

The persons who know 'Economic chemistry' can become rich without practicing any wrong methods or losing any moral values.

'Economic chemistry' is nothing but the capability and skill of converting a commodity that has 'lower value' in the society into a commodity that has 'higher value' and demand in the society.

In medieval ages, people used many process to convert the lead into gold. (This can be seen in Vemana History). Of course, they failed in their attempts.

But these attempts laid foundations to the modern chemistry.

The conversion of 'lower values' into 'higher values' can be seen in computers also.

The silicon that is used in computers is obtained from 'sand'!

Intellectuals like Bill gates and others converted their ideas and thoughts into products and services and practiced the economic chemistry.

Now Let's Discuss How One Can Become Rich

The first point to pile up money is to earn more money than before!

A small question arises when we say more money than before is that do we mean double?

Three times? OR

Ten times?

OR Thousand times?

If you have the eligibility and capability and sincerely work for a company giving your best, then you can earn more money!

If you are shaped into a valuable person than before, then also you can earn more. This is the secret to become rich!

It's not surprising that the capacity to earn more will increase the capabilities, intelligence and creativity in you. The skills and talents in you that very few people possess, when used creatively, will definitely result in more money.

For example- why does a doctor earn more than a driver?

The answer is simple-

In our life a doctor gives more valuable service than a driver!!

We find many persons who have learnt driving in few hours, where as we find few doctors who study hard for many years, compete many competitions and renew themselves.

If you want to earn more than what you are earning now, you have to ask yourself the following questions:

"How can I give better services for the company I work in?"

"How can I help my company earn more profits in a shorter period?"

"How can I reduce the expenditure and increase the quality of the company?"

"How can I suggest new techniques by which the company can become more efficient?"

With these questions in your mind, daily you have to increase the knowledge, skills of your field and try to increase your potentialities.

It is very important to possess self-development and self-education for every person!

The main principle to increase your earnings is-

You shouldn't ask your company to raise 50% of your wage without increasing 50% of your potentiality.

In this regard, you ask the following questions-

"How can I increase the value of my work to 10 times or 15 times?"-

When you are able to do it automatically your earnings will increase.

You have to increase your 'value' more than what you have now!

Do you want to be 'Best'?

Or do you want to exhibit the 'Best' in you??

To become 'Best' means Perfection.

To exhibit 'Best' means Excellence.

The persons who want to be 'Best' remember
their mistakes and think about them.

The persons who want to exhibit 'Best' will
set right their mistakes and learn lessons from them!

It's up to you, how you want to be.....

The second step to pile up money- to protect the earnings!

After earning some money how do you maintain it?

A simple method of maintaining your earnings –

Spend less than what you earn and invest the remaining money. This way you can become rich in the long course of time.

It's surprising that some people earn a lot, but don't have control on their expenditure. With this, they remain same in their status even after many years.

The important principle to pile up income:

Invest some percent of your income in any means!

When there is a clear understanding between the wife and husband regarding the monthly expenses, then there won't be any chance of arguments and quarrels.

The third step to increase your wealth

First, you decide what you need.

Without aim, you can't throw an arrow!

To become rich one should not only has to earn more than before but must learn to invest it carefully. The interest earned from the investments should be reinvested again.

Many of us spend our income only for our life style. We even like to use our increased income to spend a costly life style but not think of savings.

The persons who achieved financial success will put aside some percent of their income and invest it in other means. Again, by investing the profits of those investments they make more money.

By doing like this, after some years they earn more money than they need and reach to a position where they don't need to work.

Now they have become the richest persons!

They got economical independence!!

It is just like a hen laying the eggs and by hatching those eggs getting the chicks. Again those chicks growing big and laying the eggs.....it's a continuous process.

If you are setting a goal (regarding
Yourself or your company) it means
You are creating a competitive atmosphere or
Competitive spirit!

A Wise Act

Suppose you have 99-rupee notes and a five hundred rupee note in your hand. Because of heavy wind, all the notes in your hand scattered and fell on the ground. Picking up which note will become a wise act?

Picking up the rupee notes those are nearer and then try to pick up the five hundred rupee note that is far away?

Or

Leaving the one-rupee notes that are nearer and picking up the 500-rupee note that is far away and then come and collect the one-rupee notes that are available??

According to the first method if you first collect one-rupee notes and then miss five hundred rupee note, you'll get a total of 99 rupees.

According to the second method if you first collect five hundred rupee note and miss other one rupee notes, you'll get a total of 500 rupees. Still if you find any rupee notes they are all additional.

So also, you should act wise with your goals. Always concentrate on big and long-term goals that yield you large profits.

It is not the quality of the wise to satisfy with small term goals and neglect important goals......

The fourth step is to safeguard your accumulated wealth

After earning a lot of wealth, one has to be careful not to lose it. With the acquisition of wealth, we are surrounded by many problems. Many people look at you with jealous, hatred and anger.

Many of them like income tax persons, politicians, criminals, police, naxals etc anticipate with zeal to grab money from you.

To tell the truth common people and middle class people hate the rich, specially if that person is one among them and grows rich!

They can't do anything to the rich but if anything happens to the rich they feel happy and will not show any sympathy.

There are some legal problems to the rich.

Therefore to safeguard their wealth, property and companies the rich has to set lawyers, financial advisers and insurance companies.

Enjoying the wealth

Some people after earning lot of wealth and enjoying all comforts still feel some emptiness in their life. They lead a life of dissatisfaction. This is because they don't find any 'meaning' in their life and feel any 'value' of it...

Generally, it happens in the lives of emotional beings and intellectuals.

Any person no matter what he earns or how happily and comfortably he lives, if he doesn't spend some amount on others there is no meaning in their lives.

- With the motive to find a 'meaning' and a 'value' to life, Birla's have constructed Temples, Subbirami Reddy is spending money on various cultural organizations and virtuous movies....
- A person who is earning money, to get a value to it or to himself, he has to use 10 percent of his income towards charity.
- Don't think that you are donating that money. Really, you are not donating that money or wasting it. You are using it to enhance your value and prestige in the people.

By donating some money in the society in the form of charity brings you a 'value'. You are buying that 'value' with your money.

So also by giving some money to others, you subconsciously feel that you have excessive amount. This feeling gives you mental satisfaction and enhances your Self-esteem.

This is what achieving success means!

"BE WHAT YOU WANT TO BE."

"You don't have a problem- you just have a decision to make."

— Robert Schuller

Success Principles

To achieve success one should know how to continue good relationship with others.

To continue good relationship with others one should know communication skills.

Communication Skills means....

- Speak less and Listen more.
- Should not be with an attitude that "Always I am right".
- Instead of thinking 'how to defeat other person' think how to understand a person.
- You should be able to tell others clearly, what you are.
- You should talk and behave in manner that "you too win and I too win", but not like "you lose and I win"

These principles are useful to succeed in the society and to win the society.

Rememberance

The persons who want to attain higher goals:

- They are with extreme optimistic attitude.
- They are always with positive thoughts.

- Without living in dreams, they show what they want in action.
- They take responsibility for their failures and not blame others.
- They put their efforts until they reach their goal.

So anybody:

Without any discontent and relentless efforts try hard then definitely they will achieve it.

With extraordinary efforts, they can achieve it in shorter period.

So remember it again-

You can achieve!

Definitely achieve!!

Don't Stop in the Middle.

The Inevitable

Sometimes conditions are unfavourable
The road you have to travel seems upright
Your money is completely exhausted
Your debts may increase
Trying to smile you may heave a sigh
Duties and responsibilities may burden you
Even then-
Don't stop in the middle,
Just relax for some time!
Life is a strange zigzag and shining path
When you are ready to achieve the success
Failure touches your hands
This is a known fact to all.
Success is like a pocket to store.
Failure is a like 'upturned pocket'
Nobody can say how near is the goddess of success
When we feel that it is far away
It may come gracefully towards you, rest on your shoulder and smile at you.
So-
Under any circumstances, don't stop in the middle
You have to struggle in unfavourable conditions only.....
Then only you will be a 'winner'!!

Is There Anything Called Fortune?

If a person achieves success in whatever task he takes up we say, "He is very fortunate!"

If a person loses his hard-earned money or wealth inherited from his fore fathers because of any disaster or loss we say, "He is an unfortunate person".

There is a belief in the world that some people are fortunate and some are unfortunate by birth. Just as some people are tall and some are short by birth…

Really is there any fortune and misfortune??

When many managers and businesspersons are observed, it is clear that they always achieve success. Some people called that success as "fortune"

But the fact is –

At the crossroads of our life when we stand thinking about which way to take, then the efforts and opportunities coming together is called "fortune"!

Efforts and the Judgements to take Correct Decisions, When Combined Together will Result in 'Fortune'!

When a person lacks these two qualities, it will be a 'misfortune' to him.

Except that, there is no 'Fortune' at all.

The word 'Fortune' itself is a foolish word.

A person's attitude to believe in 'Fortune' will not yield any success.

To tell the fact, the below mentioned aspects will help a person to achieve success, who is striving hard for success.

- ❑ His inbuilt potentialities

- His efforts
- Opportunities coming together

There are difference of opinions between men and women regarding success and the feelings regarding the success.

- When men achieve success they feel that it is achieved only because of their ability, it means only because of their talent and intelligence.
- But women are not like that, they feel that success is achieved not because of them but because of the external factors like fortune and others cooperation.
- Your forth-coming success depends on how you are applying the reasons from the present success.
- If you think that, your are achieving success only because of your talents and efforts, this thinking will enhance your self-confidence and further lead you forward to achieve many more victories.

But one thing-

There is also a convenient with the feeling of 'fortune'.

When you believe that only because of 'fortune' you'll achieve success, this belief generates 'optimistic' attitude.

'Optimistic' attitude encourages towards achieving success. (For many detail read the chapter 'optimism' from this same book-)

But there is a bad quality in the person who believes in fortune is that by chance if he encounters a failure simply he will think that it's his bad luck but never try to analyse the factors that are responsible for that failure.

Definitely, this factor will stand as an obstacle to achieve success.

Success never comes because of the 'fortune'. It comes only through following and practicing the principles of success.

If you want a promotion, earn money, achieve success simply you shouldn't keep quiet by believing in God or fortune and putting your burden on them. You have to develop the qualities that are necessary to achieve success and become a 'winner'!

Fortune – Belief

Fortune is only a belief. The persons who don't have confidence on themselves depends upon fortune.

- There is a close relationship between the mind and the body. If the belief is on the positive side, it will yield positive results.

When it is on negative side, it will yield negative results. It may be regarding their health or success.

- ❑ Black magic, palmistry, fortune and zodiac signs all these aspects exploit the 'belief' in man.
- ❑ Gossip and curse also work depending upon the 'belief'.

In British Medical Journal, there is a case history regarding the belief. It is like this:

Once a foreteller tells to a five-year girl "when she reaches the age of 43 she will die". These words are strongly imprinted in the girls mind.

After 38 years she celebrates her 43rd birthday. After one week of celebration, she has to undergo an operation. By the time, she is a mother of five children.

It's a very minor operation.

The night before the operation, she said to her sister "I have got 43 years. Now I don't live, with this operation I will die".

(This sister is also present when that woman is foretold about her death in her childhood days)

One hour after operation, she has lost her complete consciousness and died.

Doctors didn't find any solution. It's not a major operation that causes her death. Post mortem report revealed that she died of internal bleeding.

Her sister told about childhood incident. Then the representative of British Medical Association examined the case and gave a report like this:

"There is no medical reason for her death. But the strong belief in her mind that she will die at the age of 43 had a great influence on her body and worked it like her fate. It's just like a voodoo death..."

So belief has that much influence on our mind! Regarding fortune, belief works in the same manner. If you take up a task confidently thinking, "Fortune is by side" or with an expectation that surely it will happen, definitely you'll achieve it.

Sometimes, after facing one or two failures the belief that misfortune is running after takes away the confidence and leads you towards more failures.

So it's not a good method to believe in the "fortune"

There is no 'fortune' at all.

Don't depend on fortune.

Efforts and the judgement to take correct decisions will only yield you achievements or success.

Some principles to follow in this regard:

- Always grab the possible opportunities (those who believe in fortune sometimes miss the possible opportunities)
- Search for opportunities
- Even if face many failures never think that it happened only because of misfortune. Learn lessons from your failures or success.
- When you win, work out which method made it possible.
- Even if you lose, try to find out the fault and where it has taken place.
- Whatever you do always try to exhibit your 'best'. Never let down your self-esteem under any circumstances.
- Regarding your future if you move forward with positive attitude definitely success will be yours....

Life is a Masterpiece!

'Victorious' means 'success achievers' as they are 'winners'. The qualities of the winners and the losers are very different from each other.

Winners get the things done according to their wishes. Losers simply yield to the happenings without any struggle. Winners take up the complete responsibility of the results. They believe that there is a reason for defeat or victory.

They believe in the saying, "You have to put your efforts for what you need but shouldn't think that someone will come and help," and they practise it in their daily life without fail.

Today what we are or what we achieved today depends upon the results of our past deeds.

Our characteristics and our surrounding climate are based without our knowledge but whether we win or lose is entirely based on our decision-making.

Up to a certain age our parents sit in the driving seat of our life, after reaching certain age and accomplishing individuality we have to sit in the driving seat of our life.

From then onwards we are responsible for all the victories and defeats of our life.

We become captives to the habits, set hundreds of limitations and live according to those limitations.

The persons, who don't take up responsibility for their actions, don't know how to behave and wait for others help comes under the persons who haven't achieved maturity.

Controlling ourselves means taking up the responsibility to display the 'best' of our mind and body.

When we are able to utilize our potentialities, wisdom, talents and valuable time means it is only possible because of our self-control. Our victories and defeats also depend upon our honesty and responsibility.

Winners not only control their lives but also their thoughts, goals and daily routines. They write their own destiny. They use their precious time for victories and never have time to lose.

Winners strongly determine to win always. They believe that as said by everybody 'fortune' depends on readiness to win and having awareness on it.

To them life is not a gamble but it's a game.

The three reasons mentioned below make them to believe that they definitely win.

1. 'Desire' – anxious to win
2. 'Self-control' – believing that only through self-control they can win
3. 'Preparation' – they prepare initially for the victory and possess the habits that are required for the victory

Without initial preparation, no one will utilise the available opportunities. It looks as if fortune favours the 'winners' but it's not a fact. Only through their efforts, they achieve the fortune.

The important aspect that brings victory to them is their – Optimism.

- Doubting people can't achieve success. Achievers of success will not doubt.
- Winners are self-made persons.
- Such people are always away from the negative attitude persons, dullards and pessimists.
- These people are attracted towards the positive attitude persons and optimists.
- 'Optimism' is like a wild fire. You can see and smell it from a distance.
- Such people like the achievers of success and like to be around them.
- These types of people never like the persons who are failures in their lives and fear to mingle with them.
- Winners have a goal and a planning. They know in which direction they are moving ahead daily.

- Winners know what they need, they do not rest until they get what they need. Always they work hard for it. Determination is their breath!
- Our life is shaped according to our thoughts, daily we make. Unconsciously, we step forward according to our thoughts.
- Winners take care of those steps to move towards their goals.
- This life, which is a gift of the nature is very precious.
- Losers don't know how to utilise their lives. They waste their lives just like a lunatic wastes the scented flowers.
- Winners know the natural qualities of their bodies. They never think that their youth is an eternal aspect and their old age as a shameful aspect.
- They know the meaning of their lives.
- Gracefully, they accept the old age or any change in their lives.
- Like a gardener, they protect their 'bodies' like a garden.
- They never fear the death, and think that in the life's journey, it's a destiny.
- They have time to look and enjoy the blossoms of Roses.
- They have time to listen and enjoy the chirping of the birds.
- They have time to look at greenery, birds, clouds, feel the cool breeze, watch the moonlight, moon, stars, sunrise, sunset and enjoy these beautiful and wonder elements of nature.
- They have time to play with children because they know that their children soon lose their childhood and grow into adults.
- They have time to console old people, as they know that their consolation fills energy in them.
- They have time to enjoy with their family members.
- They have time to listen to music.
- They have time to read books because they know that books are like vehicles that carry them towards knowledge. Through books, they can travel many places and acquire vast knowledge.
- They do not avoid hard work. They spend the required time to finish any work. They know that to live in this materialistic world, they have to work and earn money for their decent living.
- They take care of their health, as they know the importance of health to enjoy good and happy life.

- ❑ Winners never live in the past.
- ❑ They learn lessons from the past incidents. They use the past as a guide and do not repeat any mistake that occurred in the past.
- ❑ They do not simply sit and dream about the far away future.
- ❑ They set vivid goals for future. Keeping those goals in mind, they step forward and bring richness and purpose to lives.
- ❑ Winners live in the present.
- ❑ They know that the present moment – this passing moment is real and it creates history. So they try to have control on 'this moment'.

Life is precious, every moment in life is more valuable. Lost moments will not come back. I want to give an advertisement under the column of "lost" in all the popular newspapers to tell the value of the passed moments.

"Lost!"

The valuable 24 hours of a day is like 24 carats of gold- in which every hour is fixed with 60 minutes as diamonds- every minute is fixed with 60 seconds as rubies- this sort of precious and wonderful golden day 'today' is lost, completely lost."

It is felt that how good it will be if the popular newspapers publish prominently this kind of "Ad" daily, to tell the readers the value of 'time'.

Winners know the value of time. Every minute they live their life, it seems as if it is the last minute.

Time is moving fast in the clock, and life is running fast. Catch the time and keep a control over all your activities. To win and achieve success in your life, there is lot of time but there is so much to be done that there is not even a minute to lose.

Life is a masterpiece, so learn to enjoy it. For that, ask yourself some of the questions mentioned below:

- ❑ "How delicately I can absorb in my family, in my profession, in my society, in my country, in my universe?"
- ❑ Treat the people as brothers and sisters. Treat the animals like human beings. Love the nature and rear it carefully. A balanced nature makes our future survival comfortable.
- ❑ Value the people you love most, show it often by giving flowers, cards and talking to them.
- ❑ Respect your parents. By making phone calls and writing letters, tell them how you love them dearly and honour them.

- Every week spare some time to spend with old people. By listening to them, you can increase your worldly knowledge and your consolation and conversation fills energy in them.
- Pay interest towards music and literature. They will revitalise your mind.
- Try to learn one or two other languages, other than your mother tongue. Study the customs and traditions of different societies and nations. While travelling in different regions, try to speak that regional language as it will be a fun and a good learning excercise.
- Show your love and care on your body by providing food rich in nutritional values and do regular exercises. Daily sleep 5 to 6 hours, because by doing so, you will increase 10 to 12 years of longevity of life.

Once again I repeat,

"Mould and Shape your Life into a Masterpiece and Enjoy it!!!"

"When all is said and done,
Success without happiness
Is the worst kind of failure." — **O. G. MANDINO**

All books available at: **www.vspublishers.com**